WEDDING PLANNING IN SIMPLE STEPS

HOW TO HAVE A DREAM WEDDING ON A BUDGET

VIKKI VALENTINE

Table of Contents

WHY YOU SHOULD READ THIS BOOK

You're engaged. Congratulations! Your head is swimming with images of the magical wedding that you have always dreamed about. You see yourself gliding down the aisle toward your beloved in a picture perfect setting. All of your friends and loved ones smile to be witnessing this happy event.

Before you get to that special day, you will have to plan a single major event and two catered meals. Your will need to:

- Determine your budget

- Select a theme for your wedding

- Choose your wedding venue

- Choose friends to be attendants

- Find your perfect wedding dress

- Research and select vendors for cake, flowers, food, and photography

How will you organize all these details? Who is going to coordinate with all the players involved? Where will you find a beautiful venue that you can afford? This book will help you plan your wedding around your top priority. It will also give you ideas about how to economize in the areas that are not your main focus, but still necessities.

Who's going to pay for this dream event? Are you a young bride with parents who are eager to foot the bill for THE social event of the season? Count your blessings! A bigger budget allows you the privilege of hiring a wedding planner. You *will* need one and the expense will be well worth the money. Don't forget Mom and Dad's pockets aren't bottomless—you will still need to cut expenses where possible.

Maybe you don't have parents to pay for the wedding and you have fewer financial resources. You will want to know how to trim your budget and still create a memorable event for you, your fiancé, all your friends, and family. This book will give you tips and ideas on how to customize the wedding that you have always dreamed of—and do it for a reasonable price.

Plan, plan, plan. Organize, organize, organize. Your wedding may seem like a tremendous chore that never ends. Don't forget that it is YOUR wedding. Regularly take time to stop and savor the fact that you are joyfully joining your life with your beloved's, and you are sharing this precious moment with those closest to you. Realize that everything will turn out okay, even if on the day of the wedding your florist says, "What flowers? I didn't know you were getting married today." To see how that crisis turned out, go to chapter 12.

I wrote this book to help you organize, simplify, and enjoy the process. Because you might need a place to record your thoughts, I've left notes pages at the end of each chapter. Use them to record your thoughts as you plan your perfect celebration.

Have a happy wedding!

CHAPTER 1. WHY HAVE A WEDDING EVENT?

Perhaps your parents or even your fiancé has suggested elopement. Should you? Elopement is a simple ceremony, perhaps only civil, with only a few people in attendance. A judge's chambers, the preacher's home, or the courthouse lawn all offer a fuss-free location. I even knew of one elopement that happened at the Justice of the Peace's office in the back of a volunteer fire department.

Sometimes a private ceremony is the best solution. If your fiancé is leaving soon for military deployment, you may have limited time to arrange a wedding. You may have fallen in love in another country and won't be returning home for a year or more. An elopement has the advantage of being quicker and easier than even a small wedding production. If you choose elopement, don't feel guilty about it. But if there is any possibility of a public wedding ceremony, consider the benefits to you and your loved ones.

ANNOUNCE YOUR MARRIAGE TO THE WORLD

A wedding draws a line in the sand. Before this date, you were two individuals conducting your own lives, not responsible for anyone but yourself. After this date, you are a couple, a family. Every decision you make will affect another person. Declare this fact to the world in a public ceremony.

In the old days, weddings were announced in the newspaper. Now Facebook, Snapchat, and Twitter declare your news to your customized list of friends. Either way, you make a public statement that this is the person I love, this is the one with whom I will share my life from this day forward.

Vowing to love, honor and cherish in a public setting shows that you are proud of your future spouse. A wedding is usually the first big event that you plan and carry out as a couple. Profess to everyone through this ceremony that you are no longer individuals, but a new, inseparable unit.

INCLUDE FAMILY & FRIENDS

A marriage of two people is actually a marriage of two families. For a young couple, it is a combination of the separate traditions of the groom's family and the bride's family. Every family has its unique customs. Your wedding is the first event uniting these cultures and will set the tone for many birthday parties, baby showers, and holiday celebrations to come.

Finding common ground is even more important to a more mature couple who may bring children from a previous marriage into the family. Include the children in the planning and execution of your wedding. It is the perfect opportunity to begin a new family unit. Choose a young daughter as a flower girl, an older one as a bridesmaid. Call on your son as a ring bearer or an usher.

2

My husband and I brought several children and grandchildren into our marriage. We called upon the older grandsons as ushers, and we included the young boys by dressing them in mini tuxedos. Even though the little ones were not old enough to serve, their formal wedding attire made for adorable family pictures.

My sister and brother are both musically talented, so we enlisted them in the choir. My future brother-in-law served as best man. My father had passed away several years before, so I was honored to have my grown son escort me down the aisle.

All these roles helped to blend our separate families together. Their inclusion not only gave them a place in the ceremony, it communicated approval of our marriage by their participation.

RECEIVE HELP

Are you completely self-sufficient and don't need help from anyone? I always tried to be. I cleaned the house, by myself and took care of the children, by myself. I Prepared dinner, by myself. Cleaned up the dishes, by myself. At the end of all that, MYSELF was exhausted. I was always afraid that if I asked for help my friends would be angry and resentful.

I found out the opposite is true. When I refused to ask for help, my friends thought I was aloof. When I did all the chores at home, my family thought I didn't need them. In my forties, I learned to ask for help from others, and I was surprised at how willing they were to give it. They rushed to my aid.

Of course none of us wants to be that person who begs and nags others to do all her personal chores. Here's my litmus test for whether you are resistant to asking for help. Picture yourself sitting in your favorite easy chair. You are relaxing with a book when you begin to feel a tightness in your chest. Pain starts at your breastbone and radiates out to your arms. You have trouble breathing. If your first thought is "I can make it to the hospital by myself," you need to learn to ask for help!

Receiving help with your wedding from family and friends has several benefits:

- Friends feel needed. Helping you makes them feel important and gives them a sense of accomplishment.
- You begin to bond early. Including his family in your planning helps them to start feeling like family.
- You get help with your wedding. With all the tasks involved in a wedding, you really do need help from others.
- You get practice in receiving. The more you practice, the easier it is to be vulnerable and accept help.
- You are blessed by seeing all the support you get from friends.

ALLOW TIME FOR ADJUSTMENT

Parents and friends may have trouble believing any future spouse is good enough for their darling: Did you date long enough? Do you really know each other? How do we know if your fiancé has good character?" Even for adult children, it is hard to think of your mom or dad being married to someone new.

Planning and conducting a public wedding takes time. This waiting period from the engagement to the wedding gives everyone a chance to adjust to the major change in your lives and theirs.

Draw children and parents into the planning process. Ask your future mother-in-law for help in selecting colors. Let your children help choose the wedding cake. Enlist friends to run wedding day errands like picking up flowers or returning rented tuxedos.

My future husband, age 58, drew his parents into participation by asking their advice. He took the time to talk with them and get their input about his impending wedding. He listened to their concerns and asked for their blessing, something he had failed to do in his 20s. I reaped the reward of a closer relationship with my in-laws because of his thoughtfulness in consulting them.

BE BLESSED

Yes, a public wedding ceremony is a lot of work. A million details compete for attention in your brain. You think of all the possible disasters: tripping as you go down the aisle, knocking over the wedding cake, forgetting to pick up the flowers. Go ahead and imagine the worst disaster. Now assure yourself that as long as you are married to your beloved at the end of the day, your wedding was a success. So, enjoy the process. Relish the planning and the details; consider the ways that you will be blessed.

Friends and family buoy you up with their support. Your girlfriend who drives 60 miles to take you to four bridal shops in one day loves you like a sister. The future daughter who creates a flower arrangement in just the right color, sees that you love her dad. Your brother, who travels 30 miles after work to chorus practice every Wednesday for a month, wants your happiness.

The best part is that even after all of your loved ones support you by their presence, they will bless you for years to come. You will relive the warmth of your wedding day every time you look back at your photo album. All the effort that you put into your special day is preserved in your pictures.

Turn back and see the sparkle in your eye the first time you beheld him as your husband. Marvel at how small the children were then, even though they seemed big at the time. Cherish the lasting images of your loved ones who have moved on.

Allow yourself to be blessed by the love and help of your family and friends. And enjoy your special day.

My Reasons for Having a Wedding Event

_____

_____

_____

_____

_____

_____

_____

_____

_____

_____

_____

_____

_____

_____

_____

CHAPTER 2. WHAT ARE YOUR PRIORITIES?

You step off the plane and palm trees greet your arrival. Family and friends gather at your island hotel. In the morning, you and your groom trek across the sand to the chapel on the beach. The minister ties the knot as you clutch your bouquet of purple and white orchids. You watch the sunset fade from orange to peach as guests feast on teriyaki beef and mai tais. After the moon appears, hula dancers and torch twirlers arrive to entertain. You savor your wedding day as you anticipate the next week of surfing and scuba diving with your hubby. Now, back to reality.

Everyone has a fantasy wedding idea. The challenge is to narrow down your wish list to the items that are most important. Is your highest priority having the ceremony at a resort overlooking a lake? Maybe you long to serve shrimp scampi to those near and dear. Or perhaps you would feel cheated unless you got married in a couture gown. Think about what is most important to you before you begin your wedding plan.

After our traditional church wedding, my husband and I sped away from the building for our secret honeymoon location. Several guests were surprised a few minutes later when they spied us in a stall at our favorite drive-in restaurant. I'd had a busy day and I was thirsty! I insisted that my husband stop so I could get my usual vanilla diet cola.

Whatever is most important to you, remember that the wedding should reflect your style. Choose the priority that is closest to your heart and be willing to compromise in other areas. But always stay true to who you are.

VENUE

Guests are seated and gazing across the lake as the waves from distant boats lap against the shore. A great blue heron swoops down and grabs a sunfish from the water. As the sun glows orange on the horizon, the bridal march emanates from a brass ensemble. The guests rise and turn to see you floating down the aisle toward your beloved.

Many venues offer a picture-perfect setting for your wedding. Options range from scenic outdoor vistas to elegant indoor arrangements. Perhaps you visualize your wedding at a peaceful lakeside location or a scented garden abloom with roses and peonies. Perhaps a ceremony staged in an elegant, historic home or an intricately designed chapel is more to your liking.

If your dream since you were a little girl was to be married at the historic Paramount Theater, venue should be the main focus of your budget. Choosing a beautiful setting creates ambiance for your wedding. Having the ceremony in a location that is dear to your heart will increase the enjoyment of your special day. Even your memories will be enhanced. Every time you look back at your stills or video, you will be reminded of the lovely locale you chose for your wedding.

RECEPTION

Your guests begin their meal with an appetizer of shrimp salad, seasonal fruit, and cheese. Friends then dig into chicken breasts in a lemon caper sauce served with warm sourdough bread. Your loved ones join in a toast to the bride and groom as servers deliver each guest a piece of almond-flavored wedding cake or chocolate groom's cake.

Nothing brings people together like sharing a meal. When that meal is a multi-course feast served in an elegant setting, the experience elevates to deep bonding. Eating together after witnessing dear friends tie the knot is a time-honored tradition.

If your greatest desire is to share a meal with family and friends at the reception, your budget should reflect that choice. Ideally, you would entertain a multitude of acquaintances. But if you have a limited budget, you will need to make compromises. An expensive meal is much more reasonable if you restrict your guests to a small number. Nevertheless, a grand wedding meal will leave a lasting impression for both you and those who attend.

CLOTHES

Your groom steps out of the alcove in a black tuxedo with peak lapels. Four groomsmen follow in matching tuxedos. All eyes turn to the back as you enter in your custom-made dress. As you draw near, guests can see the intricate beadwork on the bodice. As you pass, they can see the cut-work lace on your trailing veil. Friends smile in approval as you sweep away to your beloved.

Her wedding is one occasion a woman can expect to be the center of attention. Knowing that everyone will be ogling every detail, some brides wish to spare no expense for the dress. If looking like a princess is your goal, you will want to cut back on other items. leaving more finances for THE dress.

You can have the wedding of your dreams. You can share your special moments with family and friends. The secret is to spend your money on the item (or items) most important to you. This book will help you to have a blessed and memorable wedding without breaking the bank.

My Wedding Priorities

_____

_____

_____

_____

_____

_____

_____

_____

_____

_____

_____

_____

_____

CHAPTER 3. ENLIST FAMILY & FRIENDS

© Vikki Valentine

My friends provided a lot of services for my wedding—for free. I never thought about it until I started writing this book. One friend, with whom my husband shared an interest in photography, took pictures for free. He even gave us a CD of all the photographs after the wedding.

Another friend from church, who did department store decorations for 20 years, volunteered her expertise. She decorated the church and the reception. She also advised me on an inexpensive way to decorate my grocery store cake. Her philosophy was if what you want costs $1000, but you can get 80% of what you want for $100, go for the 80%.

My best friend and her amateur chef husband contributed the rehearsal dinner. The whole dinner! They bought all the food, and with an army of teenage volunteers prepared, served, and cleaned up afterwards. Some of the best pictures from my wedding are of the sumptuous dishes my culinary friend prepared.

Many other friends contributed smaller, but essential, services. A college friend picked up the flowers, or tried to—more about that later. My brother and sister sang in the choir. My future daughter picked up the cake.

Your family and friends love you and want to be part of one of the most special days in your life. Let them! Don't have an attitude of entitlement and expect everyone else to foot the bill. But if someone wants to help you, allow them to do so. Use it as a chance to practice your receiving skills.

SERVICES

Everyone has a special talent. Some are gifted with a beautiful voice, some with cooking skills, and others with organizational ability. Doubtless, your friends and family have a wide range of talents as well.

Even a modest wedding and reception is a complicated production. If you have a friend who is willing to serve as wedding planner, take her up on it! Mobilizing your volunteers and vendors is a job that requires both organizational and diplomatic skills.

Perhaps you have a talented seamstress in the family. I started sewing when I was about ten years old. I made most of my clothes through high school. So, when I was 17 and my sister decided to get married, I made both her bridal dress and my bridesmaid's dress. I was honored that she wanted me to make her dress, and felt an essential part of the wedding by providing such an important item.

Your friends are varied and so are their talents. My friends contributed photography, singing voices, venue decorating, and catering. You may have friends skilled in flower arrangements, hair and makeup, or musical performance. Be open to whatever services they offer, and allow them to help with your wedding.

BORROWS

Something old, something new, something borrowed, something blue, and a silver sixpence in her shoe.

This Victorian rhyme prescribes the items that a bride should wear at her wedding for good luck. Let's take it as a blessing for a bride to borrow useful items for her wedding day.

Borrowing from a friend should be considered a privilege and never an entitlement. A friend's treasure should be treated with even greater care than we give to our own. Such attention is reflected throughout history. In the Old Testament, if a man lost a borrowed item, he was required to pay it back twofold. Taking a more modern source, the Emily Post Institute advises, "Borrowers do have an obligation to replace items they break or lose." So, be extra cautious with items loaned from friends.

That being said, friends' unique possessions are a great source for essential wedding needs. Physically, the largest borrow would come from a friend who offers his home or land for your ceremony and reception. Although there is little chance of losing someone's house or garden, there is great potential for damage. If you have a friend kind enough to provide a venue for your wedding, be sure that you and all your helpers treat it with great respect. Even go so far as to appoint monitors at the reception to watch for vandalism—whether through intent or negligence. Also, don't forget to provide a staff to clean up afterward. Since the bride and groom leave before anyone else, you need a trusted leader for this task. Nothing leaves a worse taste in the mouth of homeowners than for visitors to trash their property.

"Something borrowed" could range from chairs and tables from your church, to a fancy getaway car from a friend, to a wedding dress from your sister. Remember that you are using someone's treasured possession, and be extra careful. Demonstrate your appreciation afterwards with a warm "thank you" note and a small gift. Sharing valued items blesses not only you as the receiver, but your friend as the giver.

ENDOWMENTS

Some of your friends (or parents) may be in a position to fulfill a wedding need with an outright gift. Remember my friend and her husband who gifted the entire rehearsal dinner to me and my husband? What a blessing!

You dream of three luscious tiers of moist white cake, interspersed with raspberry filling, topped with fresh red roses like the ones your fiancé gave you on your first Valentine's Day together. A baker in the family can help make your wedding cake dreams come true. Even if your baker is not in a position to provide the whole cake, maybe he could give you a reduced rate. He might even be willing to prepare it for the cost of materials.

Tender, juicy brisket with that hint of smoke flavor made Bob the top grill master in the family. Handmade yeast rolls with a slice of real butter ensured Sarah's place in the culinary hall of fame. If you have friends talented in food preparation, they may be willing to help with a do-it-yourself wedding dinner. Depending on how many people you plan to feed, a few friends could prepare the entire meal. For a large gathering (over 20), you could ask more people to bring smaller quantities of food, making it easier for everyone.

A diamond solitaire mounted in an Art Deco style setting adorns the third finger of your left hand. You couldn't be more thrilled that Granny agreed to give your fiancé the ring that your grandfather gave to her. Many families have heirloom jewelry from previous generations. These treasures add sentiment and family tradition to your modern day union. Granny's gift frees you from buying an expensive engagement ring and includes you in the stream of ongoing family history.

Sharing talents or treasures allows your family to demonstrate their love for you. Giving you things of value is another way of putting their stamp of approval on your fiancé and your wedding. Receive their gifts with gratitude and show your appreciation with a note of thanks for their generosity.

ERRANDS

Not every friend has a one-carat diamond to contribute to your ring or an antique car to loan for your reception getaway. But anyone can help with one of the myriad errands necessary to pull off a successful wedding.

Most errands occur right before or right after the wedding. The closer you get to the ceremony, the more help you need running errands. Recruit any volunteers or willing bodies to help during this critical time.

Before the ceremony, enlist drivers to ferry out-of-town guests from the airport. If you have a lot of family coming in, you may need more than one chauffeur. The day of the wedding, you need delivery drivers to pick up the cake and flowers and bring these items to the venue. Cake and flowers can both suffer from a rough ride or being left in a hot vehicle. Be sure to discuss with your friends how to assure the cake arrives un-cracked and the flowers un-wilted.

After the ceremony, your husband will spirit you away on your honeymoon. You need trusted friends who will finish up at the reception in your absence. Someone needs to pack up leftover cake, pick up trash, and put up the tables and chairs. If you hire caterers, cleanup is part of the service. If the reception location was a gift, however, make sure you don't leave your hosts to clean up alone afterward.

Designate someone to return rented formal wear. Ask your mom or maid of honor to pack up your wedding dress and take it to your house. Any gifts brought to the ceremony need to be delivered there as well.

Not every gift has a monetary value. Allow your friends to give of their time and lighten your burden. You will always remember how their kindness made this day even more special, and they will too.

ADVICE

Friendly words of wisdom can guide you through sticky situations. Your experience is an important teacher, but why not learn from others' experience, too? Include your friends in your wedding plans by asking their advice. You are not obligated to use every idea, but you will honor them by asking.

Ask friends, "What was the best part of your wedding?" Learning what made other weddings special gives you potential memory makers for your own. My future husband took a cue from another couple for a unique receiving line. Instead of lining up at the reception to shake hands, we greeted each person at the end of the ceremony. We went down the aisles, dismissing each row of people in turn. Each guest received a hug from the bride and groom as they left the church. We both treasured greeting and thanking each person as they filed out.

Be sure you also ask, "If you could redo your wedding, what would you do differently?" Going through months of preparation, then the pins and needles of the big day, puts a perspective on what is really important. Call on the experience of your friends to help you know which areas are "must do" and which are "let it go."

SAMPLE SPEECH

Friends picking up relatives at the airport, a cousin altering Mom's wedding dress—help is essential for a low-cost event that includes everyone. Be ready to receive gracefully, but remember to ask graciously.

Chances are that your family and friends will be anxious to help out. Remember that it is always someone's choice to assist. Don't expect others to give you help or financial aid; simply allow them the chance.

The bride should seek help from her family and friends, and the groom from his. It is probably best to approach friends individually or as a couple. Don't pass out a sign-up sheet at the next family reunion and expect everyone to pitch in or else! Below is one way to approach those from whom you want help. You don't have to use these exact words, but be sure to keep an "attitude of gratitude."

> I'm getting married! You are a special person in my life and I wanted to tell you in person. We have chosen a public ceremony. We really want to include all our family and friends in the wedding and reception. Our goal is to keep things simple, but planning and carrying out an event like this is a big job. We would appreciate your help in any way possible. If there is anything that you would like to volunteer for, we'd love to have your assistance. I value your friendship and even if you aren't able to help, I would be honored to have you attend my wedding.

Family and Friends Who Can Help

Chapter 4. How Much is in the Budget?

The good news is that I finally got her to agree to a small wedding.

© Vikki Valentine

Now that you have taken time to think about what is most important to you, it is time to check your bank book. How much money do you have to spend on your dream wedding? Check through all of your possible income sources before your make your final plan.

PARENTS' CONTRIBUTION

Begin with a heart-to-heart talk with your parents. You will be excited about your engagement and want to share your good news with all your friends. That is perfectly natural. But don't wait too long to tell your parents. Try to inform them the day you become engaged or the day after.

Nothing is worse than hearing important news about your child second hand. Before you announce your upcoming nuptials to the Facebook world, give your parents a call. They, and you, will be glad you did.

Allow some time for your parents to adjust to the idea of your marriage. Then arrange to meet them privately. This is not the time to bring your fiancé into the family council. Save that for later.

Tell your parents that you want to have a public wedding. You want a ceremony and reception celebrating your new life with those who are closest to you. Assure them that you do not want a blowout that will bust the budget.

Thank them for all they have done for you in the past: food, shelter, clothing, education. Inform them that they are under no obligation to pay for your wedding. You are making out a budget, however, and need to know if they'd like to contribute.

You will likely receive a positive response. Acknowledging their past contributions, and not having an attitude of entitlement, says a lot about your maturity. They will want to help you—after all, they are your parents! Be grateful for whatever they offer.

Maybe financial aid from your parents is out of the question. If they are strapped for cash, they probably won't be able to help you. Or perhaps you are a mature bride like I was, and your parents are no longer living. Either way, you can honor your parents by paying for the wedding yourself.

MONEY IN SAVINGS

After getting a commitment from your parents, take a look at your own resources. Maybe you have a childhood savings account that has been drawing interest for years (however paltry that interest may be). Extra points for you! Now is the time to tap into it. Perhaps you have a good job and can manage a pay-as-you-go plan. Excellent!

If you don't have loads of cash lying around, you will have to make do. Don't forget to check for miscellaneous income sources. Do you have a savings account for a project you have abandoned (backyard shed, converted garage, college education)? Maybe you can repurpose those funds. How about old jewelry that you could sell? Especially if it is from a previous relationship, now is the time to get rid of it!

LONG ENGAGEMENT

Maybe you don't have rich parents or a secret stash, but you have lots of patience and self-control. (If so, how did you end up on this planet?) Or your intended may be stationed in the military half a world away. Or one of you is in college with a couple years left to finish that degree. You have no choice except to wait.

Use this time to your advantage. Save all you can towards the big day. Open a savings account specifically for your wedding. Determine an amount you can save each month and stash it away. Don't worry if you don't meet every goal. Even if you save only a little each month, you will still be ahead when it comes time to pay for the ultimate party reception.

MAKE PAYMENTS

Advance planning is always on your side. You may not have lots of ready cash, but your wedding is still months away. Use those precious months to your advantage.

Decide on your flowers, cake, photographer, and reception in advance. Meet with each of the vendors and see if any of them are open to a payment plan. Everybody likes a big chunk of cash, but the chances are your vendors will accept protracted payments, especially if you are planning to pay off the balance before the big day.

DON'T GO INTO DEBT

Now is the time to stop and remind yourself of your goals. What's really important? Number one, you want to marry the love of your life and live happily ever after. Number two, you want to share this life-altering event with those nearest and dearest to you. Those two goals are the bottom line; every other goal is secondary.

Are you having trouble paring down your guest list? Do you really want your third grade teacher to share your special day? Stop and think—when is the last time you saw her? If it hasn't been since, well, third grade, you may want to send her an announcement card instead of a wedding invitation.

Sometimes old rivalries resurface and you have to do battle with them. Your sister got married last year with four bridesmaids. You feel you need five bridesmaids because everybody knows you have more friends than your sister. Pause, take a breath. Do you really have five best friends? Personally, I only have one. Even if you have more, other good friends can still take part by singing at the service or serving cake. Save yourself the trouble and expense of all those extra bridesmaid dresses.

Maybe budgeting is not your strong suit. Have you had trouble spreading your paycheck to meet all the bills? Can't seem to balance your checkbook? (I am one of the few people on this planet who still does this.)

Get help for attaining financial health. Many tools exist to help you set financial goals, create a budget, and pay down your debt. One resource I recommend is Dave Ramsey. I have no affiliate marketing relationship with his organization. My husband and I took his class, Financial Peace University at our church. I know that it helped us to get financial control early in our marriage. I have many friends who have benefited from his advice, too. This no-cost tool will help with your personal budget. https://www.everydollar.com/app/#/sign-up/daveramsey

Give yourself the gift of entering your marriage debt free. It will be a great way to start your new life. Your future spouse will be relieved that you aren't bringing debt into your partnership.

Budget Notes

CHAPTER 5. MAKE YOUR PLAN

You choose to have an event that includes your family and friends. You know which element is your top priority. (If not, review chapter 2.) You have assessed your resources, both financial and labor wise. Now, it's time to convert your wishes into a game plan.

LIST AVAILABLE FUNDS

Your overall goal is a fun family gathering to celebrate your new marriage. You want to include as many people as possible. You can have a joyous wedding with next to nothing if you put in a lot of work, but even a moderate budget is easier to pull off. Come up with a reasonable goal for your total cash outlay.

Review the financial information you gathered in chapter 4. Use the list below to remind you of possible money sources. Then, write down all your assets and estimate the amount you can save before the wedding. Then total all your funds.

Parents - bride $_____

Parents - groom $_____

Current accounts - bride $_____

Current accounts - groom $_____

Future Savings   Months x savings per month $_____

Total $_____

REVIEW WEDDING ESSENTIALS

Consider what you want the wedding to include. Review the following list and cross out any items that you do not want or need. Fill in items that are being donated. Note family and friends who have volunteered to help with each item.

Need	Donor	Volunteer	Funds
Wedding Venue	_____	_____	_____
Reception Venue	_____	_____	_____
Officiant	_____	_____	_____
Wedding Musicians	_____	_____	_____
Reception Musicians	_____	_____	_____
Bridesmaid Dresses	_____	_____	_____
Photographer	_____	_____	_____
Dress & shoes	_____	_____	_____
Invitations	_____	_____	_____
Flowers - wedding	_____	_____	_____
Flowers - reception	_____	_____	_____

Rehearsal dinner venue	_____	_____	_____
Wedding cake	_____	_____	_____
Groom's cake	_____	_____	_____
Hair & makeup	_____	_____	_____
Tuxedos	_____	_____	_____
Wedding Rings	_____	_____	_____
Engagement Ring	_____	_____	_____
Wedding decorations	_____	_____	_____
Reception decorations	_____	_____	_____
		Total	_____

DISTRIBUTE FUNDS

Compare your available funds with your wedding essentials. If your funds exceed your needs, you are good to go! More likely, your needs exceed your funds. Time to reassess.

Remind yourself of your top priority. Are a high percentage of your assets designated for that need? Or did some other item creep in and suck up all your funds? Rethink your top priority.

Did you choose the item (venue, reception, clothes) that is most important to you? If so, redo your budget to appropriate the needed money to that area.

Some items are essential, but don't have to use up a lot of funds. Consult the chapters on individual items like venue, dress, and flowers for ideas on how to handle these things inexpensively.

Now you have your budget game plan. Make copies and give them to your fiancé and your volunteer wedding coordinator (maybe your mom or best friend).

Refer to your game plan to remind yourself what these fund allocations are. Add any volunteers or donations to the list as you go along. Keep in mind that your wedding plan is a work in progress. You will have to make adjustments along the way.

Remember: plan, but be flexible.

Notes on Financial Plan

_____

_____

_____

_____

_____

_____

_____

_____

_____

_____

_____

_____

_____

CHAPTER 6. CHOOSING A WEDDING VENUE

Think back to your childhood fantasies of the perfect wedding. They were probably all tied to a special place: an elegant chapel with colored light streaming through stained glass; an outdoor locale with hills and a setting sun in the distance; or perhaps a dance floor surrounded by twinkling lights where you have your first dance with your new spouse.

The average couple indicates their desire for a special place with their pocketbook. Most wedding budgets dedicate almost half of the available funds for the venue (and catering). So, choose carefully.

Discuss location expectations early on with your fiancé. Nothing is worse than planning an elaborate chapel wedding for 500 and then finding out your intended wanted to get married on the beach with only close family and friends. It's much easier to compromise before you start putting down deposits.

VENUE – PRIORITY OR NECESSITY?

Your goal is to have a lovely wedding without exceeding the budget. You accomplish that by prioritizing and spending accordingly. Review chapter two to clarify which part of your wedding has priority.

Since most couples spend half of their budget on the venue, it will be hard to not make that your priority. You do have options, however. If your dream is a bead-encrusted designer dress, you will need to find ways to save money on the venue.

First ask yourself: Is the wedding venue a priority or a necessity? If it is your first priority, you will have more funds to work with; you can choose from the priority venue options. But if some other item has priority, you will need to look at the necessity options—the less expensive alternatives.

Each wedding plan is unique. If the venue is not number one, you may have a friend willing to let you get married in their historic home. Lucky you!

Venue Variables

Do you want a ceremony location for 12 people or 200? Do you want the ceremony, reception, and rehearsal dinner all in one place? Are you willing for your guests to drive from the ceremony to the reception? Do you want the venue to provide the catering or do you prefer to arrange that yourself?

All of these questions are necessary because venue choices vary greatly. It's very difficult to compare venue alternatives head to head because they do not offer the same sizes, options, or services. But because there are so many types of venues, you can surely find what you want if you search for it.

Priority Venue Options

You've decided that a memorable venue is the most important item in your budget. You'll have fun choosing from all of the exciting options. (Well, maybe not FUN, but it is amazing how many choices you have.) The following are a few of the non-traditional venue options available to the bride who wants her guests to have a unique experience.

The following information is based on venues available in or near Fort Worth, Texas. At the end of each listing are sample search engine terms (Google, Bing, Yahoo, Ask, etc.) to help you locate similar venues in your area. Note: If you want to get married in a different city than where you do the search, add the city name at the end of the search terms.

I found that I got better search results even in my own town if I added the city and state name to the search. If you are unhappy with your search results, try adding your location. You may weed out unwanted listings.

HISTORIC HOME

Does your hometown have interesting historic homes? Historic properties are generally over 50 years old, are relatively unchanged over time, and have some architectural or historical significance. Many old homes are listed in the National Register of Historic Places. But even those that aren't listed can be of interest. Preserved homes are usually those built by the wealthy of their time and have opulent features, interesting architecture, and a great location for your wedding.

Location
1899 Cattle Baron Mansion

Number of People
70 inside, 125 outside

Includes
50 folding chairs, six serving tables, changing room for bride

Cost
$1450 for 4 hours or $2400 for 10 hours plus $500 refundable damage deposit

Advantages
Beautiful setting with some chairs and tables provided

Disadvantages
Limited size; must hire outside vendor for catering; may need to rent more chairs

Search Terms
Wedding venue historic houses

BED & BREAKFAST

A bed & breakfast offers a homelike setting for your wedding. Many B&Bs are repurposed historical homes, so you can celebrate your wedding with a touch of the past. Due to the smaller, more intimate size, B&B innkeepers often require couples to rent every room in the house for the night of the ceremony. This increases the overall cost, but also adds to privacy, since no other rental guests will be there.

Location
Bed & Breakfast with outdoor garden

Number of People
10 in parlor, 150 in garden

Includes
Ceremony coordinator, officiant, tables, chairs, sound system, bridal photo session, honeymoon suite, in-room breakfast

Cost
$995 for one-hour, 10 guest ceremony/reception, includes cake, punch, bouquet $3395 for garden wedding and reception for up to 150 guests, includes all B&B suites, catering not included $300 refundable damage deposit. Discounts for active military, police/firefighter, minister, or weekday ceremony

Advantages
4-level rock water feature in garden, secluded outdoor setting but close to town

Disadvantages
Must rent all rooms for weekend weddings, no DJ or live band after 10 p.m.
Must have TABC bartender or uniformed officer if serving alcohol

Search Terms
wedding venue bed and breakfast

NATIONAL OR STATE PARK

If you are looking for a rustic wedding locale, there is nothing more rustic than the raw beauty of the great outdoors. United States National Parks capture the diverse experience of nature ranging from 7993-foot-deep Hell's Canyon to 20,320-foot-tall Mount Denali. Parks also provide the opportunity to experience geysers, caverns, and waterfalls. Don't forget your state parks. They offer unsullied views of the natural features that made your home state famous.

Location
State park encompassing a 120-mile canyon

Number of People
169 at deluxe pavilion, 54 at day use pavilion

Includes
Deluxe pavilion: table and chairs, heat and A/C, water, electricity, kitchen, restrooms
Day use pavilion: fire ring, outdoor grill, nearby restrooms

Cost
Deluxe pavilion - $1000 per day plus entrance fee, $500 refundable deposit
Day use pavilion - $250 per day plus entrance fee, $250 refundable deposit

Advantages
Breathtaking views

Disadvantages
All attendees must pay park entrance fee, if holding event within park. Ceremony cannot block trails or access to facilities

Search Terms
wedding venue national park or wedding venue (your state) state park, example: wedding venue Texas state park

NECESSITY VENUE OPTIONS

You dream of exchanging vows in a historic church filled with stained glass windows, walking down the aisle surrounded by the sounds flowing from a two-story pipe organ. You long for a custom-designer wedding dress that flatters your shape and highlights your curves in all the right places. You want to serve your guests gourmet delicacies that will forever etch the experience of your reception in their memory banks.

Unfortunately, your budget may not allow you to have ALL of those things. If a gorgeous wedding venue is not your budget priority, you still have many options. Take a look around. The settings that are close at hand are likely your most economical ones too. Perhaps you can create a beautiful, inexpensive venue in your own home, city, or friend's property.

YOUR HOME

Nothing is more intimate than your own home. Inviting guests into your home to witness you tie the knot is the ultimate in private hospitality. Your home already contains the stamp of your personal taste and style. You will have to rent or borrow some items such as tables, chairs, and maybe even a tent for the backyard to get it ceremony ready.

Location
Your house

Number of People
Approximately 40 inside for 1500 sq ft house
125 outside in 30' x 30' rented tent

Includes
Your own tables and chairs, your facilities (kitchen, bathrooms)
Your yard

Cost
Rentals per day: white chairs $3.50 each, bridal arch $44, stage $48
Tent rental - $675 per day for 30' x 30' tent, $270 delivery and set up, plus city tent permit

Advantages
Intimacy and privacy of your own home
No cost to rent venue, no time limit for decorating or ceremony

Disadvantages
You are responsible for all cleaning, setting up, and decorating
May have to rent equipment; you suffer loss for any damages

Search Terms
party rentals

CITY PARK

You pay city taxes if you own a house. If you rent, part of what you pay your landlord goes for city taxes. You are helping pay for city services and facilities; why not take advantage of them? Options vary from city to city, so check it out. You may find some gems in your hometown that you hadn't seen before.

Location
City park gazebo

Number of People
Approximately 20

Includes
Two benches, electricity

Cost
$20 per 3 hours for city resident, $40 for non-resident

Advantages
Surrounded by landscaping, trees, and creek running through park

Disadvantages
Probably need to rent chairs and bridal arch
not private because people still have access to nearby areas of the park

Search Terms
city of (your city, your state) park rental, example: city of Fort Worth, Texas park rental

FRIEND'S RANCH

Are you a little bit country? If your soul soars at the chance to gaze at distant hills, hear the wind ruffling through the trees, and breathe in the fresh air, you belong in the country. Do you have friends who own a ranch or a rural vacation property? Perhaps they would allow you to use their location for your outdoor wedding. If they are willing, you could consider use of the ranch as their wedding gift to you.

Location
Friend's ranch

Number of People
Only limited by your friend's boundaries

Includes
Outdoor location for wedding

Cost
Rentals per day: white chairs $3.50 each, bridal arch $44, portable toilet $175

Advantages
Setting of natural beauty, private

Disadvantages
You are responsible for all cleaning, setting up, and decorating
May have to rent equipment, you should compensate friend for any damages

Search Terms
party rentals

TIPS FOR SUCCESSFUL VENUE SELECTION

Your wedding day will be an event you always remember. Use the following tips to ensure a wedding venue you will be happy with. Careful preparation will increase the chance that your ceremony goes smoothly. Remember: plan, but be flexible.

- Book your venue as early as possible, even if you only have two months to plan, like I did.

- Put a deposit down to hold reservation if venue is very popular.

- Remember convenience costs; all-inclusive venues cost more.

- Don't forget the cost of tables and chairs if your venue is for location only.

- Make accommodations for elderly or handicapped guests at an outdoor setting. They may need a place to sit in the shade or require wheelchair-friendly access.

- Ask how soon before the wedding you can come to decorate.

- Schedule your wedding off season, during the week, or in the morning to save money (most places).

Venue Notes

CHAPTER 7. WHERE TO HAVE RECEPTION (AND REHEARSAL DINNER)

"I'LL BE RIGHT BACK, HONEY. I FORGOT TO BUY PUNCH FOR THE RECEPTION!"

© Vikki Valentine

Your wedding reception is the opportunity to party with your friends and celebrate your new marital status. The ceremony sets a serious tone as you commit your life and faithfulness to the one you love. The reception is the time to have fun and show off your party skills.

Because both the reception and rehearsal dinner usually include a meal, this chapter addresses both. Almost any place you choose to have the reception could accommodate your rehearsal dinner, too. But this doesn't mean that you want to have them at the same place.

Maybe you chose an all-inclusive venue, such as a vacation destination, hotel, or your church. In that case, the wedding, reception, and rehearsal dinner could all be at the same place. Some venues, however, are ceremony-only or reception-only. So, all three events may be in different locations.

In general, a rehearsal dinner is a smaller event. Your primary consideration is finding food you like and space to eat. A private room is good so you feel comfortable making after-dinner speeches.

For a reception, you may be serving a meal like the rehearsal dinner. The difference is you also need room for the traditional reception activities: cake cutting, bouquet throwing, and garter tossing. If you are really partying, you will need a dance floor, too.

RECEPTION – PRIORITY OR NECESSITY?

Did you choose a scrumptious meal shared with family and friends as your priority? If so, the reception is the place to spend the big bucks. The good news is that the more you spend on food, the more services come with it. Receiving your guests at a fancy restaurant includes not only indulgent food, but wait staff to serve it, and porters to clean up afterwards.

Maybe the reception is a necessity for you because you chose to invest more funds in a lovely dress. You still have options. Hosting a meal for a large group is a major challenge, but you can do it. Perhaps a friend gifted you with his talents in meal preparation. Maybe you could choose a less expensive restaurant or caterer. You could even choose the tradition that I grew up with—skip the meal altogether and have a cake and punch reception.

RECEPTION VARIABLES

Are you a do-it-yourselfer? Or do you prefer to make one phone call and have someone else take care of the details? You can be as hands-on or as detached from the execution as you want. How much of your time and money you spend on your reception depends on several things.

Obviously, if you want to prepare all the food yourself, it's going to take more time. But that isn't the only option. How many people you invite affects your expenditure, too. You could choose to entertain a large group at less cost if you prepare it yourself. Alternatively, you can choose a fancy restaurant if you keep the number of attendees small.

The services that restaurants and caterers offer also vary a lot. Some have an attractive location where you show up and they do all the work. Others allow pick up and you provide the setting up, serving, and cleaning up. Sometimes the same vendor will offer either type of service. You have many options to choose from; keep searching until you find the service that is right for you.

PRIORITY RECEPTION OPTIONS

Do you want the lobster Thermidor or the filet mignon? Maybe your budget isn't quite that big, but it's fun to dream. If the reception is your priority, you have a lot more choices. If you have a fun reception location in mind, you may ask your guests to drive a little out of the way. Or you may have the luxury of caterers delivering and serving food in a facility adjacent to your wedding venue. Either way, you have choices. The following are some indulgent options for your wedding feast.

The information below is based on venues available in or near Fort Worth, Texas. At the end of each listing are sample search engine terms (Google, Bing, Yahoo, Ask, etc.) to help you locate similar venues in your area. Note: If you want to get married in a different city than where you do the search, add city and state name at the end of the search terms.

Upscale Restaurant

Nothing says fine dining to me more than a well-cooked steak. Maybe you prefer seafood. Either way, an upscale restaurant is the ideal way to treat your guests to a sumptuous meal. The price is higher, but all you have to do is show up and they cater to your every dining need.

Location
Steak restaurant

Number of People
12 in glass enclosed room
36 in fully curtained room

Includes
Meal, private location, flat screen TV for presentations (slide show)

Cost
$56 per person for filet mignon, salad and dessert
$76 per person for shrimp appetizer, salad, lobster bisque, filet mignon, dessert

Advantages
Delectable meal with set up and clean up included

Disadvantages
Probably more suited to rehearsal dinner, no dance space, expensive

Search Terms
upscale restaurants with private rooms (your city, your state)

City Museum

Looking for something to appeal to the artist or scientist within you? Local museums often have private areas that can be rented for special events. Sometimes you can rent access to a particular exhibit or even the whole museum. Major cities have an abundance of museums. But don't forget to check out the smaller cities in your area. They may have their own quaint museums that you can rent out for less money.

Location
Science and history museum

Number of People
125 in special events room

Includes
Seating, drop-down screen, catering

Cost
$500 room rental plus $1500 minimum catering expenditure

Advantages
Unique setting
Can add private planetarium showing for $750

Disadvantages
Tempting to purchase access to entire museum for $11,000

Search Terms
museum event venue

VACATION DESTINATION

Destination weddings became an all-in-one alternative for brides and grooms in the 1970s. Couples were looking for new ways to make their wedding a unique experience for family, friends, and themselves. Even though these weddings take place at exotic locations, they often cost less than traditional wedding and reception sites. The average traditional wedding in the United States costs $35,329, whereas the average destination wedding costs $28,000. You may not be planning to spend that much on your nuptials, but a multi-day wedding vacation may be the way you choose to celebrate with your most intimate friends.

Location
Lake cottage estate

Number of People
30-40 indoors

100 outdoors

Includes
Venue, furniture rental, decorations, photographer, flowers, officiant
Day-of wedding coordinator, hair dresser, makeup artist
Catering, staff, DJ/live band, tent rental
Overnight accommodations for up to 10 people (5 guest rooms)

Cost
$15,000 for 30-40 guests
$39,000 for 100 guests
Full wedding planning services available for additional $1500

Advantages
All inclusive, can have ceremony on boat dock with lake as a backdrop

Disadvantages
Friends have to travel to wedding
You must choose which of your family/friends get to stay overnight

Search Terms
destination wedding packages

Necessity Reception Options

OK, paying for a five-course feast for your 100 closest friends is not your idea of a good investment. Even so, nothing unites people like eating together. You want your wedding meal to be the beginning of a lifelong friendship between your family and his. So your reception will be more on the frugal than the extravagant side. It still works as the first major event shared by your separate clans.

Your modest reception is no less important than an expensive one. Saving money means that your location will be more basic, and you will have to do more of the work yourself. This is a great opportunity to invite his Aunt Janice to work alongside your cousin Sharon as they create the world's best wedding cake. Afterwards, the world will be a better place thanks to their collaboration.

COMMUNITY CENTER

An indoor location with kitchen and bathroom facilities is a real plus for a reception. No need for an alternate bad weather plan because your guests will be warm and dry inside. Most cities have a community center. Larger cities normally have several. Shop around the nearby cities. Even for a non-resident, the rental fees are very reasonable. You may find a quaint little gem to host your event in a nearby town.

Location
Community Center

Number of People
75

Includes
Indoor facility with tables, chairs, kitchen and restrooms

Cost
$30 per hour (resident), $60 per hour (non-resident), 3-hour minimum
$15 per hour mandatory rental attendant fee
$75 refundable damage/cleaning deposit

Advantages
Close to home
Can hire outside caterer or provide your own

Disadvantages
Must schedule around city recreation activities, no alcohol allowed

Search Terms
(your city, your state) rental facilities

YOUR CHURCH

Many brides dream of a church wedding—why not a church reception? Most churches, even the smaller congregations, have fellowship halls. The hall is used for classes, church dinners, as well as baby and wedding showers. So they come equipped with tables and chairs, and usually a fully functioning kitchen.

Members are often allowed to use the facilities for free as long as they return the room to its original configuration. If you don't have a home church or at least one close to your wedding locale, you may be able to rent one as a guest. Since clean-up is a major issue, you will probably need to pay a security deposit.

My future husband and I had a lovely rehearsal dinner at his church. A chef friend generously donated his cooking talents. The teens from our church acted as wait staff and cleanup crew. Because it was at a private setting, we had plenty of time to visit with friends after the meal.

Location
Church fellowship hall

Number of People
100-125 depending on table configuration

Includes
Tables, chairs, fully functioning kitchen

Cost
$150 for members, $200 for non-members
Two attendants at $50 per hour for chair setup
$250 refundable security deposit

Advantages
Designed for serving meals to large groups, plenty of parking

Disadvantages
Catering must be arranged separately
Many churches only allow members to use facilities

Search Terms
church fellowship hall for rent (your city, your state)

CASUAL RESTAURANT

Do you and your fiancé have a favorite restaurant? Maybe your eating place has a private room that you can use for the reception or rehearsal dinner. Some restaurants will allow you to order from the regular menu and use the room free for your get-together. Other restaurants require ordering from the catering menu, and charge you for use of the room.

Don't make any assumptions! My favorite restaurant has a large, glassed-in room separated from the main dining area. Since they served my favorite food (barbecue) and they had a private room, I thought it would be perfect. However, when I called to reserve it for the rehearsal dinner, they said Friday nights were one of their busy times and they wouldn't let me use the room. Recently, I found another local barbecue restaurant that does offer their private room. Whatever you are looking for, keep searching. Your solution is out there.

Location
Barbecue restaurant with private room

Number of People
24

Includes
Separate seating area for your party

Cost
Free with minimum $100 food purchase

Advantages
Private, free room, can reserve ahead of time

Disadvantages
Not enough room for a large group

Search Terms
casual restaurants with private room (your city, your state)

TIPS FOR SUCCESSFUL RECEPTION SELECTION

Take the time to sit down at your rehearsal dinner, gaze around the room, and be thankful for all the people who love you. So many people have come together to make your dreams come true. Then on your wedding day, savor all of the friends surrounding you at the reception. Enjoy greeting each one and express your gratitude for their support.

Careful planning beforehand helps you to relax and relish the event. Keep these tips in mind to help you create a worry-free celebration.

- Don't forget to schedule time at your location for decorating and cleanup.

- Have a backup plan for bad weather if your event is outdoors.

- Consider the season when choosing the locale. Even though an outdoor, Texas wedding in August is unlikely to be rained out, the heat will be unbearable!

- Compare costs carefully. Add up the expense of all the extra rentals required for a DIY (do it yourself) reception (tables, chairs, dishes, tablecloths). In some cases, an all-inclusive option is cheaper.

- Recruit more helpers than you think you need, if you choose DIY. Better to have too much help than to have guests arrive at a reception that's not ready.

- Don't forget to buy punch for the reception.

Reception Notes

_____

_____

_____

_____

_____

_____

_____

_____

CHAPTER 8. WHO'S BAKING THE CAKE?

A beautiful cake is in the eye of the beholder. Do you want a traditional three-tier, white-on-white wedding cake? Or do you long for something more unusual, like a tower of delicious donuts? Maybe your groom wants his cake to be a declaration of team loyalty to his alma mater, complete with fondant football and school mascot.

Another question: Is your cake a priority or a necessity? Go for that "ice princess meets super hero" custom cake if your budget allows. On the other hand, a tighter budget dictates a less extravagant cake. Whether your cake is a priority or a necessity, you have many choices in either category.

For my future husband and myself, the wedding cake and the groom's cake were necessities. I cruised down to the bakery department of the local grocery store. Not new to making wedding cakes, they had a book with pictures of cakes to choose from. After consulting my fiancé, we chose a traditional white wedding cake and a chocolate groom's cake.

At our reception, we were both puzzled by lots of chocolate loops piled on top of the groom's cake. He told me the cake looked like it was crawling with snakes! The cake tasted good, however, and our guests enjoyed it. So we didn't worry about it. Later, I studied the craftsmanship and said, "Honey, those are hearts all over the cake." Whatever cake you choose, make it memorable.

PRIORITY WEDDING CAKE OPTIONS

Pull out all the stops for that priority wedding cake. Bakers can provide an impressionistic painting, recreate your invitation motif, or print photos of your courtship. If you can dream it, a baker can put it on a cake and tie it all into your color scheme.

You aren't limited to a traditional cake anymore. Create a unique cake to reflect your hometown, hobby, or romance. Make your reception even more memorable by choosing an option that isn't cake at all. Any dessert is a possible candidate for a special wedding treat. Think about what makes your relationship unique and use your imagination.

CUSTOM BAKERY

Custom bakers make wedding cakes every day. They are the experts and you will pay more for their skill. If you choose an elaborate, expensive cake, you will be glad for the baker who knows how to construct and deliver a beautiful cake that also tastes good.

Speaking of taste, ask about a cake tasting. Many bakers will schedule a time for you to sample available cake flavors while discussing decorative design. Some bakers conduct a tasting for free; others will apply the tasting fee to the total cost of your cake.

Description
Custom Wedding Bakery

Cost
$4 to $6 per slice, $400-$600 for a cake to feed 100 guests

Advantages
Custom design, delivery and cake setup included
May be cheaper than your caterer

Disadvantages
Expensive; number of choices may be overwhelming

Search Terms
Custom Wedding Bakery

YOUR CATERER

What could be more convenient than having your caterer provide your cake also? Many caterers are one-stop shops, providing dinner, cake, and flowers, too. If your caterer provides the cake, you don't need to make separate arrangements for delivery, setup, and serving. Unless you desire an exotically unique cake, your caterer can provide the grand confection, and you have one less vendor to hire.

Description
Caterer that provides food for reception who also provides cakes

Cost
$3.50 to $5 per slice, $350-$500 for a cake to feed 100 guests

Advantages
Convenience; have many of the same options available as custom baker

Disadvantages
Caterer may buy from custom baker and mark up to sell to you,
No advantage if your reception isn't catered

Search Terms
Wedding Catering Baker

Barista Coffee Bar

Coffee aficionados love starting their day with a customized latte or cappuccino containing just the right dash of flavor and foam. What better way to treat your guests than with a dedicated barista who will create each individual's coffee dream? While other brides are serving cake and punch, you can give your friends an unforgettable coffee bar experience.

Description
Barista who serves custom coffee to guests
Vendor sets up coffee bar, serves guests, and cleans up afterwards.

Cost
$600 for two baristas to serve up to 100 guests for two hours

Advantages
Unique reception option, guests are usually allowed more than one coffee
Can be combined with dessert bar described under necessity options

Disadvantages
Not everyone loves coffee. Expect about 65% of your guests to have coffee.

NECESSITY WEDDING CAKE OPTIONS

So, you spent all of your money on a one-of-a-kind, bead-incrusted, mermaid wedding dress. Or maybe you chose a steak and lobster dinner at a downtown hotel for your reception. Either way, it's time to think about the cake and your money is gone.

Relax. Not every gorgeous cake option costs bundles of silver and gold (both of those cost extra on cake, so maybe you should skip them). Lower-cost options include bakers who work out of their home, grocers who also bake, and cake choices that aren't cake at all.

COTTAGE BAKERY

Some bakers choose to bypass the expense of a commercial kitchen, separate building, and industrial equipment to work out of their homes. They can offer baked goods at a lower cost because they don't have the overhead of bigger operations. Many advertise online or have Facebook pages. Ask your friends if they know any cottage bakers they can recommend.

Note: Cottage bakeries have been legal in Texas since 2011. Home-based cooks may sell items from a short list of homemade foods. Baked goods are included in the allowed list, but cream fillings are not. Check your state laws.

Description
Bakery operated in a private home. Cottage bakers can advertise, but they cannot sell over the internet. Deliveries must be in person.

Cost

$2.50 per slice for one tier, $250 for 100 guests

$3.00 per slice for multi-tier, $300 for 100 guests

Advantages

Lower cost, more personal transaction

Disadvantages

Cottage bakers are not required to be inspected by the health department

Search Terms

Cottage Bakery (your city, your state)

GROCERY STORE BAKERY

Many grocery stores have bakeries that produce professionally decorated cakes. It isn't only about marshmallow bunnies eating orange frosting carrots anymore. Stores with large bakeries have books of designs from which to choose. Most will do a custom design if you bring in a picture and complete description of what you want.

They can also custom match your colors from a fabric swatch. Don't expect gold or silver layers or marbleized effects, but do expect a nice, customized cake. The cake options are good, but the price is the best part.

Description

Large bakery at your local chain grocery store

Cost

$140 for 3-tier cake for 134 guests

Advantages

Good quality cake at moderate price

Disadvantages

No high-end custom choices (gold, silver, marbleized)

Search Terms

(Store) wedding cake (your city), for example: Walmart wedding cake Fort Worth TX

CAKE ALTERNATIVES

Many brides forego the cake. Instead of a traditional three-tier cake, you can offer a different dessert option. If you still want cake, consider a cupcake sampling. Offer your guests a variety of cake and frosting choices.

Another option is a mini-pie bar. Or try a donut tower for the fritter lovers. The tower shape makes a good centerpiece. You could even offer brownies or an ice cream cake.

Many smaller desserts are less expensive than a cake and give you the opportunity to try more flavors. Cupcakes from a custom baker will be more expensive than the same number of treats from your grocery store bakery. Bypassing the expense of a large cake could allow you to choose small designer treats from your custom baker.

Description

Individual servings of desserts, anything from cupcakes, pies, or brownies to donuts, cookies, or ice cream cake

Cost

$295 for 100 designer bakery cupcakes, $56.58 for 100 custom grocery store cupcakes
$300 for 100 mini pies
$150 for 100 cookies, $112 for 100 custom grocery store cookie cupcakes
$200-$400 for 100 gourmet donuts, mini-donuts $1.50 each
$200-$240 for four ice cream cakes to feed 100

Advantages

Unique alternatives to wedding cake, less expensive, easier setup, can offer more variety
Good in combination with barista coffee bar

Disadvantages
With several flavor choices, guests may eat more (mini sizes better for sampling)
Non-traditional choice if you always dreamed of a wedding cake

Search Terms
Cupcakes (your city), for example: Cupcakes Fort Worth TX
Mini Pies for sale (your city)
Cookies for sale (your city) Gourmet Donuts (your city)
Ice Cream Cake (your city)

TIPS FOR SUCCESSFUL CAKE SELECTION

The wedding cake is your chance to do the traditional cake-cutting and bride/groom cake-feeding you dreamed about. Or maybe you want to be less traditional and are looking for cake alternatives.

Either way, you want the cake or its substitute to be the showpiece of your reception—a reflection of your style. You also want to avoid disasters and get the most value for your money. Cake selection is important: After the bride, the cake is the most photographed item at the wedding. Use the following tips to facilitate the best cake experience.

- Ask your baker if you can decorate the cake with fresh flowers. They may be cheaper than other decorations. And make sure to ask your florist for extra flowers.

- Arrange for your cake to be served at 75 degrees or below Even if your wedding is outdoors, serve the cake inside or in the shade.

- Cut one inch into the cake in a wedge shape for the traditional bride/groom cake-feeding. A small piece is much easier to handle.

- Tell your baker if you want to save the top tier of your cake. He can give you a box for storage.

- Save money by getting a small display cake for looks and a large sheet cake for feeding your guests.

- Add one or two fake foam layers in your cake to get the look of a large cake at a lower price.

- Schedule each baker's cake-tasting on a different day. Spreading such sampling out allows your palate to reset after a few flavors. You also avoid an over-tasting bellyache.

- Ask for cake baker recommendations. Whether you choose a custom caterer or a grocery store, not all bakers are created equal. Ask friends, social media circle, or bridal forums for testimonials.

- Ask bakers if they loan dessert tiers for your cupcakes, cookies, or mini pies. That may save you the expense of buying your own.

- Pie- and cake-filling options are seasonal. Spring and summer choices are cherry, peach, apricot, and strawberry. Fall and winter options are apple, gingerbread, peppermint, and pumpkin.

- Expect to pay more for fondant than buttercream frosting. Fondant is required for intricate shapes or photos printed on the cake.

- Remember that an intricately decorated cake is more expensive than a simple one. A larger cake is not necessarily more expensive.

Wedding Cake Notes

_____

_____

_____

_____

_____

_____

_____

_____

_____

_____

_____

_____

_____

CHAPTER 9. WHAT DRESS SUITS YOUR FIGURE?

It's all about the dress. The most dramatic moment of any wedding is when the groom and all in attendance turn to see the bride walking down the aisle. Her hair clings tightly to her head in sparkling curls. Her makeup highlights her beautiful face and eyes. But nothing is more striking than the dress that hugs her body in all the right places. Yards and yards of netting and lace create a frame for her happy face as she glides toward her intended.

Naturally, you want to get it right. You want to choose a dress that highlights your best features and hides your flaws. To do that, you need to understand your figure type and different dress types.

First, look at the different figure types and suggestions for everyday dressing. Read through the descriptions and determine which type is closest to your figure.

Next, armed with knowledge about your own shape, match one of the wedding dress types with your figure. The right choice will take your look beyond "What a nice dress" to "She looks fabulous!"

FIGURE TYPES

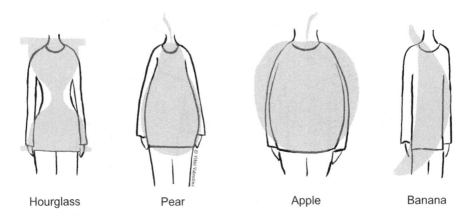

Hourglass   Pear   Apple   Banana

A pear, an apple, a banana—current figure terminology sounds about as sexy as a fruit salad. These terms, however, are relatively universal. If you learn which category you fit, almost any sales clerk can help you find a dress to suit your type.

Think of dressing for your figure as a search to find balance. Most people consider an hourglass figure to be highly attractive. Picture Christina Hendricks or Marilyn Monroe. The classic 36-24-36 figure is desirable because it is perfectly balanced. The curves above the waist are matched by the curves below the waist.

Unfortunately, only 8% of women have an hourglass figure. The rest of us have to figure out how to bring our asymmetrical shapes back into equilibrium. There are many factors to consider—like height, weight, and waist (long or short). But mostly you need to call attention to your lesser features to balance out your more prominent features.

If you have the small bust and big hips of a pear shape (like me), wear bright colors and patterns above the waist. If you are well endowed in the chest with a flat bottom (like an inverted pear shape), wear bright colors and patterns below the waist. This is an oversimplification, but it illustrates the point. Add embellishments to the smaller half of your figure to balance it with the curvy part of your figure.

HOURGLASS

Wouldn't every woman like to have an hourglass figure? Yes and no. Yes, lots of curves are very sexy. Getting a va-va-voom reaction every time you walk in a room is ego boosting. No, some women prefer a slender, modern look.

Bold prints and patterns or frilly ruffles aren't really for curvy women. An hourglass shape is already in balance so big accents on top or bottom throw your figure out of balance. Dress in solid colors to best show off your curves. If you want to appear slimmer, wear vertical stripes and tops that end below hip level.

Description
Curvy bust and hips, small waist

Other names
X-shape

Accentuate
Slender waist with fitted tops and jackets

Minimize
Avoid ruffles and bulky blouses to prevent looking top heavy
Avoid pleats and embellished jean pockets to prevent looking bottom heavy

Best Feature
Overall shape

Celebrity examples
Beyonce, Marilyn Monroe

PEAR

I think of my pear shape as one half of an hourglass figure. I have a slender waist and curvy hips. All I have to do is draw attention to the top half of my figure and it gives the illusion of a balanced figure. This fashion trick obviously works for Jennifer Lopez. Although she is a classic pear shape with a pleasingly rounded bottom, many fashion articles claim she has an hourglass figure. Way to accentuate the positive, J Lo!

Description
Wider in hips and thighs, smaller busted

Other names
Triangle, spoon

Accentuate
Top half with a colorful blouse, big scarf, or necklace

Minimize
Bottom half with dark, solid pants or skirts

Best Feature
Most pears have a small waist, wear belts, and fitted jackets

Celebrity examples
Jennifer Lopez, Michelle Obama, Kelly Clarkson

APPLE

A woman with an apple shape has those all-important endowments on top. She is larger in the bust and shoulders, and the eye is naturally drawn to the top half of her figure. One of the bonuses of this body type is that it usually comes with shapely legs. Balance out your top-heavy shape by calling attention to your legs. Wear a short skirt with print hose to equalize the bottom half with the top half.

Apple figures overlap with inverted pear figures. Both are well endowed in the bust and have slender, shapely legs. The difference is in the waist. Apples have a wider waist and look best in longer jackets that draw the eye down in a slimming effect. Inverted pears look good in a belted outfit with bolder colors on the bottom half of the figure.

Description
Wider in bust and shoulders, narrower bottom

Other names
Inverted pear, inverted triangle, cone

Accentuate
Bottom half with a print skirt or jeans with back pocket accents

Minimize
Top half with dark, solid tops

Best Feature
Ample bust, shapely legs, wear V-neck tops and above-knee skirts

Celebrity examples
Angelina Jolie, Catherine Zeta-Jones, Cindy Crawford

BANANA

A banana figure type is straight up and down with few defined curves and no waist. The good news is that 46% of women have your figure type. So, finding clothes designed for you should be easy. The other good news is that calling attention to your middle with a wide or flashy belt gives the illusion that you have a waist.

Most fashion models have a banana figure. Since the majority of clothing styles are created for your figure type, you are the envy of all your friends!

Description
Shoulders, hips, and waist all about the same width

Other names
Rectangle, ruler, athletic

Accentuate
Dividing line between top and bottom; color or texture changes give illusion of curves

Minimize
Lack of curves with belt or sash to create waist

Best Feature
Slender figure, can wear body-hugging styles

Celebrity examples
Taylor Swift, Keira Knightly, Catherine Middleton

DRESS TYPES

Now that you know your figure type it is time to apply that knowledge to your wedding dress selection. Dress styles are practically unlimited. You can choose or special order anything you want. There are, however, a few basic styles that cover the most common types of wedding dresses.

Look for the style that is most flattering to your combination of figure, face, and height. Fortunately, several of the basic styles are flattering to almost any figure. That's what makes them classic. Enjoy your shopping and don't stop until you find the one that flatters your shape.

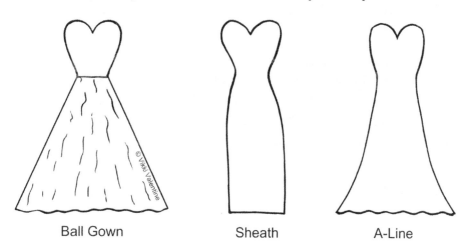

| Ball Gown | Sheath | A-Line |

BALL GOWN

The yards and yards of fabric in a ball gown dress allow you to float down the aisle. At the reception, the full skirt swishes romantically while you dance. Cinderella and Jackie Kennedy were both belles of the ball in their princess style gowns. Fulfill your girlhood fantasies of elegance by choosing a ball gown wedding dress.

Description
Fitted bodice, voluminous skirt, usually strapless

Other names
Princess

Best for
Almost all figure types

Advantages
Full skirt hides wide hips on pear, balances bust on apple, and creates curves on banana

Not Good for
Petite figures; full skirt can overwhelm small frame

SHEATH

Princess Charlene of Monaco successfully showcased her trim swimmer's body in a form-following, sheath wedding dress. Sheath dresses reveal a bride's curves without being too body hugging. The classic, lean lines make for an elegant dress. The long flow flatters both petite and athletic brides. A sheath is a good choice if you want to show off your great figure, but not too much.

Description
Straight dress; subtly follows body curves from bust to hips; straight skirt below hips

Other names
Column

Best for
Banana, hourglass, petites

Advantages
Long straight lines lengthen petites; sash at waist gives banana curvy look

Not Good for
Pear; accentuates wider hips

A-LINE

If there is a universally attractive wedding dress, it's the A-line. Not as full as the ball gown, it still has a princess look and feel. It evidently worked for Princess Kate. She wore an A-line gown when she married Prince William. The fitted bodice of an A-line highlights (or creates) a bride's upper curves. The full, flowing skirt gives a dramatic look and hides lower figure flaws. A great dress for any bride.

Description
Fitted through bust and waist; flares from waist to a full (not voluminous) skirt

Other names
Modified A-line is fitted through hips and less forgiving of figure flaws

Best for
All figure types

Advantages
Elongates short and full figures; balances pear and apple; adds curves to banana

Not Good for
Bride desiring a figure-revealing dress

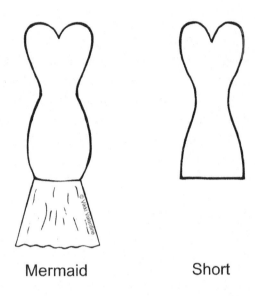

Mermaid   Short

MERMAID

If you have curves that you want to show off, the mermaid dress is for you. A stunning outline on an hourglass, it looks good on a banana figure also. The form fitting style magically adds curves to a slender, straight figure. But beware if you are an apple or pear and need to balance your figure: a mermaid dress is unforgiving.

Description
Body-hugging dress, fitted from bust to thighs, flares out from knees to full skirt at floor

Other names
Trumpet; less fitted than mermaid

Best for
Hourglass, banana

Advantages
Shows off curves

Not Good for
Pear, apple, or anyone not willing to reveal entire shape

SHORT

When Yoko Ono wed John Lennon, she was completely non-traditional in a short white dress and sneakers. Not all short wedding dresses are that informal. Lace and pearls look good on a short dress too. If your wedding is at a vacation destination or an intimate affair with a few friends, you may opt for a less formal, short skirt. Hey, if the short wedding dress worked for Cindy Crawford, it can work for you too.

Description
Short dress that ends above or just below the knees; can be any style; less formal

Other names
Tea length, falls between ankle and knee

Best for
Depends: if A-line style, all figure types

Advantages
Shows off great legs; freedom of movement

Not Good for
Bride desiring a formal dress

CURRENT STYLE

Wedding dress styles have changed over the years. Queen Victoria made the most impact when she diverted from current fashion and wore a white wedding dress instead of the traditional red or black. Brides have been wearing white ever since.

Other style changes are more temporary. In the 1910s, brides wore long-sleeved, loose-fitting dresses that were easy to dance in. Roaring 20s brides desired slim-fitting flapper dresses. The 1950s brought romantic ball gowns with full skirts. The 1970s brought elaborately styled and decorated long sleeves. The 80s eliminated the sleeves with strapless gowns. Kate Middleton reintroduced the sleeves in her 2010 wedding to Prince William.

On and on it goes, bouncing from one trend to another, and then back again. Styles are in constant flux, but one thing is timeless: A wedding dress that is perfectly suited to the bride completes her dream look. Not only that, a well-chosen dress continues to flatter through the years as you revisit your special day in pictures.

In the end, the most stylish dress is the one that looks good on you.

Notes About Best Dress for Your Figure

CHAPTER 10. BUY YOUR DREAM DRESS ON A BUDGET

You know what type of figure you have and what style looks best on you. If not, read chapter 8 for information on determining your basic shape and reviewing the available dress styles.

Now it's time to get down to shopping. If you were born to shop, this is where the wedding prep gets fun. If you are like me, however, dress shopping is about as much fun as watching an infomercial on cellulite. Not to worry, both the shopaholic and the shopaphobic need a plan, and that is what this chapter is about.

WEDDING DRESS – PRIORITY OR NECESSITY?

Decide first if you want to spend a large chunk on the dress or economize. If the dress is your priority, allocate more of your funds for its purchase. If something else is your priority (beautiful venue or large reception), your dress becomes a necessity.

Making the dress your priority means you get more choices. More funds mean you can customize your wedding dress with the lace veil and beaded train you've been dreaming about. Pay professional tailors to precisely fit your gown to your shape. Enjoy a personalized fit you could never get in a dress bought off the rack.

Choosing to save money on your dress does not mean that you will have a cheap-looking dress. Open your mind to more options and unconventional solutions; you may find a deal on a gorgeous dress.

The cartoon above portrays my friend's experience in buying a necessity dress for her second wedding. A single mother of three, she needed to be frugal in every category. Not only was she short on funds, being a working mom she was also short on time. On her chosen shopping day, the phone rang. Her sister was called in to work and needed an emergency babysitter for two children.

My friend was not only a hard worker, she was a good sister, so she said yes. Off she headed to the thrift store with five kids in tow. Her mission was to find a dress THAT afternoon. Otherwise, she would be wearing her work uniform to get married in. She pulled into the store parking lot and spotted a sale sign, "Everything $5."

She unbuckled the kids and dragged them into the store. She searched the racks for the right dress. The kids crawled under the clothes racks looking for lost coins. She found something she liked only to discover it was the wrong size. One child stole a coin from the other and ran to the far side of the store. The second child gave chase at high volume.

She looked on the next aisle. One of the kids asked to go home. She said no. The child flopped on the floor and started screaming. She located a dress she liked and checked the size. Just right! She grabbed the dress and headed for the cashier. The baby started screaming and she picked him up.

As she reached the checkout stand, she saw the small print on the sale sign: "Everything $5 *except wedding dresses*." She dropped the dress on the counter and gave the cashier a hopeful look. He observed her, the screaming baby, the flopping child, and the fighting children. He said, "Please lady, you can have it for $5!"

WEDDING DRESS VARIABLES

The type of dress you choose depends on the venue and the season. Be prepared to spend lots of money or time to obtain a lovely dress.

Your venue dictates whether you need a formal or informal dress. An evening wedding at a country club calls for a formal dress. A ceremony on the beach suggests an informal frock. Formal will usually cost more than informal.

The season affects your garment choice, too. Choose appropriately. You will shiver at your ceremony if you pick a strapless gown for a winter wedding in South Dakota. Conversely, you will sweat if you wear an ermine jacket in sunny south Texas.

All dress options are affected by time. Select your venue first, so you know what type of garment to purchase. Then choose your dress as soon as possible. Both salon and homemade dresses require time for fittings. Less expensive options like thrift store or rental need time for alterations. The sooner you start, whatever your option, the better.

Priority Dress Options

You've decided it's all about the dress. Enjoy your customized dress shopping and all of the designer options. Look online at current gowns so you have an idea of what you want before you go in. Make an appointment to ensure someone is available to help you. If your desires are very specific, bring pictures and fabric samples to show the sales person.

Designer Salon

This is the place where you get to have it your way. Custom shops can mix and match bodice, skirt, and train from different dresses to create your desired combination. Or they can custom sew a dress from scratch. Tell them what you want and allow them to make suggestions in the areas you aren't sure about.

Description
Bridal boutique that carries pre-made designer dresses or creates custom designs

Cost
$1100 to $7000

Advantages
Can create exactly the dress you want; have a garment worth saving for posterity

Disadvantages
Very Expensive, longer lead time

Search Terms
Bridal shop, designer salon wedding dresses

MEGASTORE

Lots and lots of choices—that's what the big bridal stores are about. Make an appointment and take two friends: one who will be honest and one who will be kind. Request the styles you want to try, but be open to suggestions from the sales associate. As you try on dresses, your friends and the salesperson will help you evaluate your options. Alterations are available for an extra charge.

Description
Bridal shop that carries wide range of pre-made wedding dresses

Cost
$100 to $1900

Advantages
Have sizes 0-26 on hand; you can try on any dress you want; alterations available

Disadvantages
No custom creations

Search Terms
Wedding dresses

SAMPLE

Bridal shops have sample dresses to try on in each style. When a style is discontinued, the sample dress is offered for sale at a discount. Most stores that carry a large selection of dresses will have many samples. Unfortunately, only the most popular sizes (6-10) are available in a sample sale.

Description

Sample sale at designer salon, megastore, or smaller bridal shop

Cost
$99 to $1000

Advantages
Deep discounts on designer dresses

Disadvantages
Limited sizes, usually 6 to 10, sold as is; check garment for tears and stains

Search Terms
Wedding dress sample sale

NECESSITY DRESS OPTIONS

If you chose a lavish reception at a downtown hotel, you probably put your dress in the necessity category. Making your dress a necessity means you'll have to spend more time than money. Reworking an heirloom dress, sewing one from scratch, or finding the right one at a thrift store will demand more hours than retail shopping.

HEIRLOOM/BORROW

Nothing demonstrates a close family bond like a daughter getting married in her mother's wedding dress. Every mother dreams of passing on her treasured wedding dress to her daughter. Maybe you have another family member or friend who is willing to pass on an heirloom gown to you. Either case will require some special care.

Styles and sizes change between mother and daughter. You may need to revise Mom's dress by removing the sleeves or raising the hem. Locate a quality seamstress and be prepared to pay a reasonable fee to alter your dress.

Description
Dress passed down to you from your mother, another relative, or friend

Cost
$55 for simple hem to $700 for major overhaul

Advantages
Sentimental value of family heirloom, low cost

Disadvantages
Dress may be too far from your size and style to be useable

Search Terms
Ask family and friends; appeal to friends on Facebook

HOMEMADE

If you can sew, you can combine a lower cost dress with custom features. Hand-appliqued lace or intricate beadwork will enhance your gown at the expense of more hours, not dollars.

As a teenager, I loved to sew. So, when my sister got engaged, she asked me to make her dress. My mom provided the creative expertise, I provided the labor. The result was a low cost dress that fit my sister's exact specifications.

Description

Dress you make from purchased pattern and fabric

Cost
$300 to $500

Advantages
Can customize; less expensive than purchasing same dress

Disadvantages
Not an option if you can't sew; inexperienced seamstress should choose simple pattern

Search Terms
Wedding dress patterns, McCall's, Simplicity, wedding dress fabrics

THRIFT STORE

Thrift stores, resale shops, and consignment stores all sell previously owned clothing. Thrift stores are often run by charities and resell donated items. If you are fortunate enough to find an acceptable dress at a thrift store, like my friend in the cartoon, it will be the least expensive option.

Resale shops and consignment stores are middle men for people reselling their own clothes. Consignment stores only accept in-style clothing in good condition. Dresses at consignment stores generally rank higher in quality and style than thrift store dresses. Look at the thrift store anyway. Like my friend, you might get lucky.

Description
Stores that resell previously owned clothes

Cost
$5 to $100 (varies with location)

Advantages
Low cost

Disadvantages
Limited selection, requires many hours to shop multiple stores

Search Terms
Thrift store, consignment store

TIPS FOR SUCCESSFUL DRESS SELECTION

- Don't buy the wrong size hoping to slim into the dress.

- Choose the venue as soon as possible. Select the dress soon after.

- Buy a dress to suit the venue: no long-sleeved, full ball gowns outdoors in Texas.

- Allow lots of time for fittings or alterations.

- Take at least two friends shopping with you. Bring one who will be totally honest and another who will soothe your battered ego.

- Make an appointment if visiting a salon or custom boutique. Request any dress or design preferences you have. This ensures availability of qualified help and garment choices.

- Eat before you go shopping. It prevents you buying a too small dress and avoids a low blood-sugar crash.

- Match your dress style to your fiancé's apparel. If he is wearing jeans, you need an informal dress. If you are wearing a ball gown, he needs a tuxedo.

- If possible, allow six months for fittings.

- Include some fabric from your mom's wedding dress as "something borrowed" if her dress does not work for you.

- Try on different styles to see what works for you before investing in material and patterns to make your own dress.

- Don't make a complicated gown, if inexperienced at sewing.

- Budget for dress customizing. Average alteration costs: $75-$250

Notes on Where to Buy Wedding Dress

_____

_____

_____

_____

_____

_____

_____

_____

_____

_____

_____

_____

_____

_____

_____

_____

CHAPTER 11. ADORNING THE GROOM

A man wants to look smart on his wedding day. Unless he is James Bond, wearing a tuxedo is not an everyday occurrence. Where do you get a tux? What other wardrobe pieces are required to go with it? Does the time of day dictate the type of tuxedo?

Maybe you don't even need a tuxedo. You can be more adventuresome. How? Dress is much more casual than it was 100 years ago. Many grooms are passing up the tux in favor of a vest and pants or even jeans and a cowboy shirt. The main rule of thumb is the formality of the groom's clothing should match the formality of the bride's.

GROOM'S ATTIRE – FORMAL OR INFORMAL?

Is the affair black tie or white tie? Traditionally in the UK, wedding attire was dictated by the level of formality. Formal dress was white tie with a tailcoat, semi-formal was black tie with a tuxedo, and informal was a tie with a suit. Proper dress was further divided into daytime and nighttime. A wedding taking place before 5 p.m. was considered daytime and required morning dress—a gray cutaway coat and gray, striped pants.

Contemporary fashion in the U.S. is far less formal. Most experts agree that a tuxedo with a black tie is appropriate for a formal occasion during the day or at night. Also, weddings are trending to informal rather than formal. Either way, you have choices.

FORMAL GROOM'S ATTIRE OPTIONS

The number one rule for the groom is matching the formality of the bride. If she wears a ball gown, he should wear a tuxedo or dark suit to complement her. Both the bride and the groom should match their clothes to the venue. A wedding in a cathedral, country club, or other upscale location calls for formal dress.

TRADITIONAL TUXEDO

A groom in a black tuxedo looks sharp at his wedding. Even years later, when family turns back to the pictures, he will still look classy. Dress groomsmen in tuxes to match the groom. Make the groom distinctive with a different vest or boutonniere. Choose a tuxedo for timeless elegance that will make him and his bride a stunning couple.

Tuxedos are also available in boy's sizes down to newborn. Consider tuxedos for your ring bearer, sons from a previous marriage, or grandchildren you want to include in the wedding party.

Description
Rental Tuxedo

Cost
$199 for tuxedo jacket, shirt, vest, pants, shirt, shoes, socks, and cufflinks
$24-$43 to purchase boy's size tuxedo newborn to 14

Advantages
Classic look (think James Bond or Cary Grant); groom's tuxedo usually free with five paid rentals; can customize colors of tux, shirt, and pocket square for different looks

Disadvantages
Expensive for a rental; conservative

Search Terms
Tuxedo rental

GROOMSMEN SAME COLOR SUITS

Give the groomsmen a little freedom of expression. Allow each guy to choose his own suit style while keeping all suits the same color. Each attendant can wear the cut that flatters him while maintaining a cohesive look with the other men in the same color. But don't go too far afield. You don't want one groomsman in a beige linen suit while another is wearing a beige tux. Keep choices close to the same style family.

Description
Variety of rental suits

Cost
$99-$192

Advantages
Groomsmen each wear best suit style

Disadvantages
May be hard to keep cohesive look

Search Terms
Suit rental

INFORMAL GROOM'S ATTIRE OPTIONS

You as a couple have an enormous number of ways to make your wedding unique. Historically, weddings took place in a church or home, with the bride in a ball gown and the groom in a tuxedo or suit. Now, weddings take place at a variety of venues, such as a garden, the beach, a park, or even a museum. Casual locales call for informal clothing for both the bride and the groom.

With informal attire, you have a myriad of choices. Anything you can dream up (or find on Pinterest) is a possibility. Match the groom and groomsmen to the rustic décor of your outdoor venue. Or copy the style of your favorite country and western star for a personalized look. Use your imagination, sparked by the ideas listed below.

VEST AND PANTS

Go a little bit casual by keeping the traditional suit without the jacket. Your buddies in vests can be color-coordinated with the bridesmaids for a united wedding party. Or stick with the classic black vest and pants with colorful pocket squares for accent. This look is a better candidate for purchasing than renting. Rentals are tied into the jacket selection.

Description

Matching vest and pants, white shirt, and tie or pocket square in one of the wedding colors

Cost
$66-$170

Advantages
Distinctive choice; more laid back; good for summer wedding; less expensive than whole suit

Disadvantages
May be hard to find matching vest and pants if not buying a jacket

Search Terms
Men's matching vest and pants

LINEN SUIT

Summer weddings cry for something cool. The bride can be cooler in a strapless dress, so why wilt the groom in a dark three-piece suit? Linen is a good option for a warm weather wedding. The loose weave allows the skin to breathe, while the natural fabric gives an elegant look. Dress it up with a color-coordinated tie and pocket square. Linen gives a dressed-up look, but allows the groom to be comfortable, even at the beach.

Description
Matching jacket and pants made of linen

Cost
$115-$350 jacket, $40-$70 vest, $50-$150 pants to purchase

Advantages
Cool, light color goes well with spring and summer colors

Disadvantages
Difficult to find for rent; may have to purchase; pieces usually sold separately

Search Terms
Suit rental linen

SUSPENDERS AND SLACKS

For a fun, dressed up (but still casual) look, try matching slacks and suspenders with a white shirt, topped off with bow ties in one of your wedding colors. You can make the groom distinctive by adding a vest and a different color tie to his ensemble. Suspenders without a jacket is cooler and a good choice for spring and summer.

Description
Slacks with suspenders in a matching or coordinating color

Cost
$50-$150 pants to purchase, suspenders $10-$43 to purchase, $10-$24 bow tie to purchase

Advantages
Inexpensive, distinctive, cool

Disadvantages
May be too casual for upscale venue

Search Terms
Men's slacks, Men's dress suspenders, Men's dress bow ties

JEANS AND COWBOY BOOTS

Bring out your inner cowboy in a pair of crisp jeans paired with cowboy boots. You and the groomsmen will be rocking it western style. Add matching western shirts to pull the group together. Top it off with cowboy hats for a complete "Men of the Ponderosa" look. Perfect for an outdoor wedding, especially one on horseback.

If you are lucky, your groomsmen already own jeans and cowboy boots. So, all you are out is the cost of coordinating shirts. When deciding which jeans to wear, remember to choose a neat pair in a dark color that is well fitted, but not tight, with no embellishments.

Description
Jeans and cowboy boots paired with matching or coordinating shirts

Cost
$60-$99 dark, dressy jeans
$63-$800 cowboy boots

Advantages
Comfortable, low cost if the guys already own jeans and cowboy boots

Disadvantages
Casual look could be expensive for groomsmen who have to buy boots

Search Terms
Men's dress jeans, men's cowboy boots

TIPS FOR SUCCESSFUL GROOM'S ATTIRE SELECTION

- Match formality of the groom's attire to the bride's. If she is wearing a ball gown, the groom should be in a tuxedo.
- Dress according to the time of day. Night is formal, day is casual.
- Choose classic looks, not trendy. Even if you dress informally, you want to look good in your wedding photos 20 years from now.
- Avoid ostentatious jewelry like wristwatches and bracelets. It detracts from your overall appearance.
- Be cool. If you are having an outdoor, summer wedding, dress in a linen suit or a non-jacket mode.

Notes on Groom's Attire

_____

_____

_____

_____

_____

_____

_____

_____

_____

_____

_____

_____

_____

_____

_____

_____

_____

CHAPTER 12. CHOOSING FLOWERS

Flowers add another measure of elegance to your wedding. The bride in her figure-hugging mermaid gown is a little more beautiful with a bouquet of red roses and baby's breath in her hand. The groom in his tailored tuxedo is a shade more refined with a rose pinned above his heart.

Mothers glow brighter with flower badges of honor perched on their shoulders.

Or maybe flowers are another source of stress—as they were at my wedding.

My wedding was planned in a quick two months, but I still ordered the flowers two weeks before the big day. We planned the ceremony to begin at two in the afternoon. Not wanting to spend an extra $50 on delivery, I sent a trusted friend to pick up the flowers at ten that morning. As my matron of honor was driving me to the church, the cell phone rang. "I don't know how to tell you this, but the florist says she has no weddings scheduled today and she's never heard of you. What do you want me to do?"

My brain searched for backup information. Did I forget to order the flowers? No, I didn't forget. I distinctly remember asking the florist to match the color of the bouquet ribbon to a cutting from my backyard tree. Did I send my friend to the wrong florist? I asked her the location of the florist. No, it wasn't wrong. It was the floral shop located on the back row of an industrial complex.

"Let me talk to the florist," I said. She came on the line. "I'm sorry, honey. My calendar for today shows four sweetheart flower arrangements and two funeral wreaths, but no wedding flowers." I protested. "I know that I ordered flowers from you. It was Saturday two weeks ago. I came with my best friend whose daughter recommended you. I brought a cutting from my backyard for color matching."

"No, no, you didn't order from me. Wait. Did you say backyard cutting? Was it purple?"

"Yes, ma'am, it was."

"Oh, my stars! When are you getting married?"

"Today. At two o'clock."

"Oh, I'm so sorry. I will get your flowers made as quickly as I can. Don't worry about picking them up. I'll deliver them for free."

So, we drove on to the church not knowing if we would be carrying our bouquets for the wedding or using them as decorations for the reception. The hour before the wedding was set aside for pictures. I posed for my bridal portrait. I posed with my groom. I smiled for the photo with the parents. All without my bouquet.

About 15 minutes before the wedding a friend rushed into the bride's room. "Here's your bouquet! I'm going down the hall to deliver the boutonnieres and the corsages." So I did get to carry my bouquet for the wedding. It was much easier to pose for pictures afterwards with something to hold in my hand.

Later at the reception a friend brought me a note. "The florist said to give this to you." As I opened the envelope, out fell a note and a hundred dollar bill. "Dear Vikki, please forgive me for forgetting your wedding."

For an extra $100, no problem!

My flower disaster might not have turned out so well. If I was unable to jog the florist's memory or I had truly forgotten to order flowers, I would have needed a backup plan. The best plan is to check in with your vendors, including the florist, one week and one day before the wedding. That way you can ensure no one forgets. Another alternative for missing flowers is to stop at the grocery store floral department. Many of them have floral designers on hand and could probably provide last minute substitute flowers.

PRIORITY FLOWER OPTIONS

Not only do you want bouquets and corsages, floral considerations include altar flowers, flower girl petals, reception centerpieces, and maybe even flowers to top your cake. It's no wonder the average couple spends $2,141 on flowers. If you can afford flowers as a priority, you get to choose more and fuller arrangements, giving your wedding and reception a truly lush feel.

FLORIST

Your first stop for lovely flowers and great expertise is your local florist. Experts in seasons and design, they can tell you what flowers are available in your wedding month and how to combine them for best effect. Be honest with your florist: tell her your fantasy flowers and your budget. She has the skill to get you close to what you want at the desired price. Ask friends for florist recommendations. It's best to hire someone with a known track record.

Description
Local florist

Cost
$175-$400 bridal bouquet, $10-$30 boutonniere, $45-$300 centerpiece

Advantages
Natural beauty and smell of fresh flowers

Disadvantages
Can get expensive if you have many attendants and centerpieces

Search Terms
Wedding florist (your city, your state); for example: wedding florist Fort Worth, TX

SILK FLOWERS

Artificial flowers have been around since the time of Marie Antoinette. When presented with a silk rose, she was so overcome by its beauty that she fainted. In the recent past, artificial flowers made of polyester looked real, but felt like two-dimensional fabric. Improvements in technology now provide soft-touch flowers which have, not only the look, but also the feel, of real flowers. An added bonus is that they last almost indefinitely and require no preservation to create a keepsake.

Description
Silk flowers

Cost
$8-$40 bridal bouquet, $3-$8 boutonniere, $20-$100 centerpiece

Advantages
Less expensive than fresh flowers; can prepare arrangements weeks or months ahead of time; can use colors not available in real flowers; no prep required to save bouquet

Disadvantages
Don't have the look and smell of real flowers

Search Terms
Silk wedding flowers

BEAUTIFUL VENUE

A botanical garden surrounds you. You can enjoy the abundance of flowers and greenery without the added cost of large arrangements. Although you may save on pew and altar decorations, you will still need to purchase a bouquet and boutonnieres. Choose real flowers to blend with the natural theme.

Description
Botanical or private garden

Cost
$175-$400 bridal bouquet, $10-$30 boutonniere
$250-$1800 venue plus deposit and chair rental

Advantages
Flowers are part of the venue

Disadvantages
Can get rained out; flowers in bloom depend on the season

Search Terms
Garden wedding venues

NECESSITY FLOWER OPTIONS

You want the splendor of a wedding thick with flowers, but can't afford the cost. The following necessity options offer some inexpensive alternatives to spending thousands of dollars at the florist. You can create your own bouquets and arrangements either from flowers that you purchase in bulk or from blooms that you grow yourself. Perhaps you will forgo the flowers altogether and choose some creative substitutes.

DIY FRESH

Don't be afraid to try do-it-yourself florals. Craft stores are full of tools and supplies needed for fashioning arrangements. The internet is teeming with tutorials that help you create anything from a one-flower bouquet to a six-foot centerpiece. If you decide to make your own wedding flowers, be sure to enlist several friends to help. Also, make it easy on yourself by keeping the designs simple.

Description
Bouquets and arrangements you create yourself

Cost
$216 for a package that makes 5 bouquets, 4 boutonnieres, 4 corsages, and 4 centerpieces

Advantages
Lower cost than florist flowers; can tailor make your own design

Disadvantages
Some skill required; you must create fresh florals day of or day before wedding

Search Terms
Where can I buy flowers to make my own bouquet

GROW YOUR OWN

If you have a green thumb and at least a year before your wedding, grow your own flowers. Harvesting flowers from your own garden is not only economical, it's environmentally friendly—no chemicals required to preserve your blooms for a long trip.

Hedge your bets by enlisting one or two friends to plant flowers along with you. Draw on your well-established garden to glean not just flowers but other greenery for filling out arrangements. Last of all, be flexible. You can never know for sure what will be blooming in the days right before your wedding. Also, be sure to have a backup plan in case of crop failure.

Description
Flowers grown in your or a friend's garden

Cost
$20 for flower seeds and fertilizer plus hours of labor each week watering and weeding

Advantages
Low cost, very personalized

Disadvantages
Bad weather or bugs can wipe out your flower crop

Search Terms
How to grow your own wedding flowers

ALTERNATIVES

Distinguish your wedding by choosing a decorative element other than flowers. Display your crafts skills with DIY décor like fabric tulips, origami paper flowers, or a cupcake bouquet. If your wedding has a rustic theme, set off your venue with burlap flowers, embellished mason jars, or bunches of wheat. Show off your glamorous side with beaded feathers, a parasol, or an embellished clutch.

Description
Non-floral bouquets and decorations

Cost
$10 origami paper flowers to $250 beaded feather bouquet

Advantages
Stand out with unique option, save money with DIY or recyclable embellishments

Disadvantages
Not for bride who has her heart set on flowers

Search Terms
Alternatives to wedding flowers

TIPS FOR SUCCESSFUL FLOWER SELECTION

- Match the type of flowers you have to the venue. Save lilies or orchids for a formal setting.

- Coordinate the type and style of the bouquet to the wedding dress. Choose a long, cascading bouquet to go with a full dress and a long train.

- Choose vases for centerpieces ahead of time. You can search for bargains and save money. Also, your selections give the florist colors and designs to use for a starting point.

- If you are arranging an out-of-state ceremony, email pictures to your florist. Advance information saves time when you finally meet with your florist in person.

- Bring pictures or your Pinterest board to show your florist the type of bouquet and arrangements you like.

- Reuse flowers from the ceremony in the reception. Large arrangements and even the bride's and bridesmaid's bouquets can be displayed on tables or stands.

- Plan on spending 10% of your budget on flowers. (Rule of Thumb)

- Choose centerpieces that are low enough to allow conversation at your reception tables.

- Hold your bouquet in one hand, below your hip for the most relaxed and photogenic picture pose.

- Choose a simple design with only one or two kinds of flowers if you are creating a bouquet yourself.
- Use hardy flowers for DIY centerpieces so that you can make and correct mistakes without spoiling your blooms.
- Accessorize bridesmaids with lanterns for a glowing nighttime effect at a winter wedding.
- Keep your real flower bouquet fresh longer by trimming an inch off the stems and placing it in water.
- Don't forget to ask your photographer to memorialize your bouquet in pictures.

Notes on Wedding Flowers

_____

_____

_____

_____

_____

_____

_____

CHAPTER 13. WHO'S TAKING THE PICTURES

© Vikki Valentine

We shouldn't have asked Aunt Catherine
to take the wedding photos.

Photos capture a moment in your life. You may be married to your beloved for fifty years, but you will never look the same as you did on your wedding day. Choose carefully the photographer who will memorialize your nuptials.

My mother, Catherine, was an avid picture taker. At every family gathering, Aunt Catherine would herd my uncles and cousins into their separate family groups. She documented every year of their lives, complete with beehive hairdos and leisure suits. She often focused on the children and neglected the rest of the family, leaving the dads decapitated. My mom photographed faithfully, but not skillfully. Make sure your photographer is not only proficient with a camera, but also gets the big picture.

Priority Photography Options

Long after your guests consume your cake, your flowers wilt, and your wedding dress shrinks (why else wouldn't it fit?), your photos remain. Tangible memories in the form of pictures endure and continue to give you pleasure over the years.

The services of an experienced photographer ensure that your vows, reception events, and group portraits are all well preserved. If the full-time services of a photographer are beyond your budget, consider hiring him for only a few hours. Another low cost option is to hire a student or less experienced photographer.

PROFESSIONAL PHOTOGRAPHER

If quality photos that capture all your special moments are a priority, hire a photographer who will do it all. Have him shoot your engagement photos. This will be a test run to see if you like his work. If your picture taker is a good match, contract him to document your wedding from pre-ceremony all the way through the reception.

Make sure you have a signed contract outlining all the services your photographer will provide with the costs. Check with his studio for contingency plans if your photographer is ill the day of your wedding. Also, insist on insurance to cover any photographer-related catastrophes. Last, ask for a disc of all the photos and the rights to reuse them for personal and social media purposes.

Description

One to two professional photographers to cover your entire event

Cost

$1195-$3500

Includes

Two photographers, 4-9 hours, all photos on thumb drive, slideshow

Advantages

All photos captured by professional, insured for mishaps

Disadvantages

Expensive, more traditional

Search Terms

Wedding Photographer your city, your state (for example, wedding photographer Fort Worth TX)

Part-Time Photographer

You may value an experienced photographer even if he is out of your price range. Consider hiring a professional for only the major events of your day: ceremony, cake cutting, first dance, etc. No need to hire someone to document your hair and makeup prep all the way to the last guest leaving the dance floor. Get the quality you want, but on a smaller scale.

Description

Professional photographer to cover a few hours of your event

Cost

$75-$300 per hour

Includes

One photographer for the time you choose; can negotiate for extras like digital copies of all pics

Advantages
Picture-taking professional; less expensive

Disadvantages
May miss some candid moments that happen outside main events

Search Terms
Wedding Photographer your city, your state (for example, wedding photographer Fort Worth TX)

STUDENT PHOTOGRAPHER

A seasoned photographer may be out of your price range, but you still want someone trained in picture taking. Student photographers are often as talented as their veteran counterparts, but they have less experience. They will shoot your wedding at a lower cost. This gives you a quality product and it gives the student another gig to add to the resume. Try to look at the student's portfolio ahead of time to see if he is a good match for the type of photos you want.

Description
College student who is studying photography

Cost
$35-$90 per hour

Includes
One photographer for the time period you choose; can negotiate for extras like digital copies of all pics

Advantages
Inexpensive; trained in latest tools and techniques; may have fresh approach

Disadvantages
Little experience at weddings; may not know how to handle unexpected situations

NECESSITY PHOTOGRAPHY OPTIONS

Every bride wants photos to memorialize the big day. Not every bride can afford to shell out funds for a professional artist. Some couples must take the frugal route. But *inexpensive* doesn't mean *lacking*. Call upon your shutterbug friends or relatives to provide documentation. Having many picture takers means that you will get multiple perspectives to round out the memories. Don't forget to appoint one main photographer to ensure that you capture all the planned shots and group pictures.

FRIEND OR RELATIVE PHOTOGRAPHER

Do you have a work chum or a first cousin who is an aspiring photographer? Hire him for cheap or free to take your wedding photos. As with any other photographer, view examples of his work before designating him your wedding documenter. Also, assign a backup picture taker in case your main choice gets sick.

Supply your amateur with the same information you would give a professional. Have a list of all of the moments and groups you want captured. Notify your wedding party of the official photographer so Aunt Sally doesn't push him out of the way to get her own shot of the bouquet toss.

Description
Friend who is a photography enthusiast

Cost
Free to $100

Includes
Whatever you agree on, hopefully pictures of all major ceremony and reception events

Advantages
Inexpensive

Disadvantages
May not get all the shots you want; unknown quality

Search Terms
Ask your friends and family for volunteers

DISPOSABLE CAMERAS

Go totally spontaneous and sprinkle disposable cameras around and ask your guests to snap their views of the wedding. A single photographer can't be everywhere. Disposables give your cousins in the back a chance to demonstrate their view of the groom stealing the garter. Best to use this method in combination with others! Leave disposables on the tables at the reception for guests to use. Hire a professional to chronicle the ceremony.

Description
Disposable cameras placed at reception for guests' use

Cost
$13 for two generic cameras to $88.99 for ten personalized cameras with names and date

Includes
Candid shots from guests willing to take pictures

Advantages
Multiple photos from different points of view, inexpensive

Disadvantages
You never know what you are going to get; guests may be too busy dancing to take pictures; some cameras will be taken home

Search Terms
Disposable cameras for weddings

WEDDING HASHTAG

Ninety-five percent of your wedding guests will have phones with cameras. Take advantage! Young people especially like to post pictures on social media. Use a wedding hashtag to harness all these bonus shots. Select a hashtag that is unique to you and your fiancé. You can brainstorm to create it yourself or search online for a free hashtag generator.

Once you select a hashtag, add it to all of your wedding literature. Include it in "Save the Date" notices, shower invitations, and your wedding website. Post signs at the reception with the hashtag and remind guests to tag pictures as they post. After the honeymoon you can search for your hashtag on social media and enjoy all the pictures your friends have shared.

Description
Label that begins with # and is added to a photo on Facebook, Instagram, etc.

Cost
Free

Includes
Searchable access to pictures guests take

Advantages
Generate anticipation for your wedding; easy way to share pictures

Disadvantages
Confusion if someone else uses the same hashtag; doesn't replace photographer

Search Terms
Wedding hashtags

TIPS FOR PHOTOGRAPHER SELECTION

- View a full wedding album of the photographer's work before your final decision. Make sure he will deliver consistent quality, not just a few good shots.
- Choose your venue before your photographer. A garden ceremony and a chapel service require different lighting and photography technique. Know your needs before you hire.
- Meet with photographers one-on-one before making a selection. Ensure that your personalities and styles will mesh.
- Insist on a contract and insurance with a professional photographer. Don't wait to be surprised that the price did not include post-processing or an album.
- Capitalize the first letter of each word in your wedding hashtag to make it readable.
- If you don't hire a photographer, assign one main volunteer to photograph all major events. Others can take photos, but make sure one person is responsible for all of the necessary shots.

Notes on Photography

General Wedding Notes

Chapter 14. Hey, Where Did My Fiancé Go?
or How Not To Be A Bridezilla

After the engagement, you float through each day. Happiness carries you through tasks as you contemplate life with your beloved. Nothing can disturb your inner satisfaction at finding THE ONE for you.

You cruise to your appointment with the wedding planner only to find the peonies you've dreamed about for your bouquet are not in bloom in your event month. You adjust and select roses instead. Your best friend sails in and announces she cannot give you a bachelorette party because she has finals the week before the wedding. You wade around that issue and decide a party two weeks ahead of time is fine. Your future mother-in-law declares that your brother-in-law can't be in the wedding unless he's the best man. You skim over that problem and let your fiancé decide.

A storm is brewing. Your sister refuses to walk down the aisle with the best man because they had a bad breakup in high school. Your mother insists on inviting Uncle Al and Aunt Nelle even though they haven't spoken for years. You are adrift in place cards for the reception dinner, trying to separate your sister and her ex.

Your head spins as you realize the red carpet in the venue clashes with your lavender and peach color scheme. Your photographer cancels and you dive for the phone to find a last minute replacement. You sink to the floor as you see the cake arrive without the peach ribbon you ordered.

You are drowning in the confetti that the wedding planner brought instead of the rose petals you chose. Your fiancé glides by. You grasp his lapels, and as you sink to the floor, scream, "What happened to the wedding I planned?"

Here are six strategies for keeping your marriage the main focus of your wedding and warding off the Bride Monster.

Don't Neglect Your Fiancé

Remember the main purpose of a wedding is to marry the person you love. Don't spend every night addressing invitations or making mints to the exclusion of your fiancé. As you get closer to the wedding, your schedule will naturally fill up. Don't forget to make time for the relationship that is the reason for the ceremony.

Brides tend to shoulder the majority of the wedding planning tasks. It's okay to decide between pink and chartreuse bridesmaid dresses without your fiancé, but do ask his input about other things. During our engagement, my future hubby was relieved that I was planning the wedding, not him. I said I would make all of the decisions unless he had an opinion on something. Taking the reins, I let him know about items as they came up. He surprised me with strong opinions in a few areas like music and tuxedos. So we worked together on those items, and I took care of the rest. He always knew he was welcome to influence a decision that he cared about.

Wedding planning lasts for a few months; your marriage will last for years. Don't let the planning overshadow the love of your life. Continue going out on dates and doing fun things together. Declare one night a week "planning free," and make it a rule not to even mention the wedding. Concentrate on your beloved and why you are getting married.

STAY WITHIN YOUR BUDGET

Don't add stress to your life by starting your marriage in debt. Remember the item you chose as your priority. Focus your finances and efforts on what's most important. Determine to use inexpensive alternatives in other areas. Yes, a liftoff of white doves would totally rock your wedding. But if you have chosen the dress as your priority, be content with a simpler ceremony.

How you handle wedding expenses sets a precedent for your future relationship. Collaborate with your fiancé on a financial plan and work together to solve any unexpected expenses. Don't get sucked in to spending money you don't have competing with other brides. Nothing brings out your inner Bridezilla faster than straining your budget and your emotions by trying to one-up your friends.

EMBRACE IMPERFECTION

When you spend six months to a year planning a three-hour event, you naturally expect it to be perfect. Don't. No matter how many dresses you tried on, photographers you interviewed, or venues you visited, we still live in an imperfect world. You may need last-minute dress alterations because your weight changed. The photographer could forget your wedding. The ceremony may move indoors because your garden venue is under a foot of water.

No matter what happens on the day of your wedding, determine that you will enjoy it. Last minute apparel adjustments will go totally unnoticed by your guests. Uncle Bill can fill in as your photographer. Try to laugh about your close-to-nature nuptials as you scurry indoors to avoid the rain. If you finish the evening married to your beloved, it was a good day.

A wise wedding planner told me to expect twenty things to go wrong. Then if you only have three or four mishaps, you'll be happy.

BE GRATEFUL

Take stock of how many people contribute, even sacrifice, to help with your wedding. Your friends, your family, even the vendors you hire, labor together to fulfill your dreams.

Your girlfriends agree to be bridesmaids: they spend money on dresses and gifts. Whenever you need an ear to bend about the latest cake frustration, companions offer moral support. Male friends answer the call to be groomsmen. These buddies show up for fittings, pictures, escort duty, and even host a bachelor party.

Mom and Dad contribute to the financial cost and try to help you with the emotional cost. Any scheme you concoct, chances are your parents are there to help carry it out. Other family members assist too. Your sister and brother, both in the wedding party, give up evenings when they could be

116

hanging out with friends. Don't forget the uncle who takes pictures or the cousin who bakes the cake.

Selecting and working with vendors can be frustrating. The planner who doesn't share your vision or the photographer whose style is a little too artsy. Chances are you have one or two vendors who connect with your goals, who have compassion for what you're going through.

Pause and count your blessings. To show your appreciation, treat your bridesmaids to a free lunch. Stop by the house to tell your parents how much their support means to you. Send a thank you note, or better yet, a tip to the vendor who smoothed the way for your special day. The more time you spend being grateful, the less time you have to feel entitled.

CHECK IN WITH FRIENDS

Wedding planning can consume all of your attention. Dress alterations crowd out free time on the weekends. Seating charts nag at you to massage them into a well-ordered, peace-inducing configuration. The relative merits of chicken Divan over chicken Marsala haunt your dreams (and your fiancé's). Check in with friends to make sure you are not morphing into Bridezilla.

The harder the truth to tell, the truer the friend who tells it. As a bride, you need true friends to keep you in balance. Schedule a lunch with your bestie for a reality check. Ask if you are heading into diva mode. Listen and thank your friend for caring enough to tell you the truth.

TIPS FOR A SUCCESSFUL WEDDING

- Respect the rules of the venue. If you think restrictions are unreasonable (for example, type of music or drinks allowed), choose another venue.

- Use the web for research. You can find a variety of wedding checklists and some are downloadable.

- Search *wedding on a budget* online for money-saving ideas.

- Pick the wedding theme early. It affects all other decisions.

- Don't talk about your wedding all the time.

- Be flexible in your requests to someone who donates an item like venue or wedding cake.

- Involve all the wedding party in the planning process. Leave no one out.

- Appreciate the way family and friends are helping you.

- Plan for half of the people you invite to attend. (Rule of thumb)

- Relax and enjoy your wedding.

Wedding Planning Notes

_____

_____

_____

_____

_____

_____

_____

_____

_____

_____

_____

_____

_____

_____

_____

_____

_____

_____

_____

TO DO List Notes

APPENDIX: TO DO LIST FOR SIMPLE WEDDING

FIRST THINGS (9-18 MONTHS)

Start wedding folder

Calculate budget

Choose wedding date

Pick wedding party

Gather guest list

Choose venue (ceremony & reception)

Book officiant

NEXT (6-8 MONTHS)

Arrange for photographer

Buy dress & shoes

Register for gifts

Buy invitations

Plan honeymoon

Select bridesmaids' dresses

Meet with officiant/plan ceremony

Book florist

Book rehearsal dinner venue

Order cake

Have dress fitting

Schedule day of hair & makeup

Choose music

GETTING CLOSE (1-3 MONTHS)

Reserve tuxedos

Buy rings

Send invitations

Get marriage license (3-90 days before ceremony)

Buy attendants' and helpers' gifts

WEEK OF WEDDING

Confirm with florist, baker, photographer

Confirm honeymoon reservations

Pick up dress

Check weather if outdoor ceremony

Assign someone to pack gifts, cake top, return tuxes after reception

Pack for honeymoon

AFTER

Send thank you notes

About The Author

VIKKI VALENTINE has been a professional writer for 20 years. She lives in Fort Worth, Texas, near her children and grandchildren. Vikki loves writing and illustrating books that make any subject simple and easy to understand.

One Last Thing...

If you enjoyed this book or found it useful, I'd be very grateful if you'd post a short review on Amazon. Your support really does make a difference. I read every review. With your feedback I can make later editions even better.

Thanks again for your support!

Made in the USA
Monee, IL
24 July 2023

39843734R00075